SONS OF THE MOON

Henry Shukman

SONS OF THE MOON

A Journey in the Andes

CHARLES SCRIBNER'S SONS
NEW YORK

Charles Scribner's Sons
Macmillan Publishing Company
866 Third Avenue, New York, NY 10022

Photographs © by Rory Carnegie

Library of Congress Cataloging-in-Publication Data
Shukman, Henry.
  Sons of the moon / Henry Shukman.
     p.   cm.
  ISBN 0-684-19204-7
  1. Andes Region—Description and travel.   2. South America—
Description and travel.   3. Indians of South America—Andes Region—
Social life and customs.   4. Shukman, Henry—Journeys—Andes
Region.   I. Title.
F3451.A5S5   1989   89-29652   CIP
918.04′38—dc20

Macmillan books are available at special discounts for bulk purchases for sales promotions, premiums, fund-raising, or educational use. For details, contact:

Special Sales Director
Macmillan Publishing Company
866 Third Avenue
New York, NY 10022

10 9 8 7 6 5 4 3 2 1

PRINTED IN THE UNITED STATES OF AMERICA

To my great-uncles and great-aunts

Contents

SONS OF THE MOON

Introduction

The Andes wall in the Amazon jungle. They run the whole length of South America beside the Pacific shore, which is a bleak strip of desert: nearly all the rivers that emerge in the Andes flow a thousand or more miles to the Atlantic rather than fifty to the Pacific. So the Andes rise up between a waste of drought and a tangle of rainforest. Not surprisingly, the mountains themselves proved the region most hospitable to the immigrant peoples from Asia who reached South America at least 15,000 years ago. These mongoloid Siberians were the forefathers of the American Indians of today.

Half way down the chain of the Andes the mountain range splits into two high ridges, the Eastern and Western Cordilleras. The ridges move three hundred miles apart, and then come together again a thousand miles further south. The area that they enclose is a bleak plateau more than 13,000 feet above sea level known as the Altiplano. Although barren and desolate, this high plateau has at times in its history been the heart of South American civilization. Two of the greatest aboriginal empires, Tiahuanaco and Inca, sprang up from it; for two centuries after the Spanish Conquest the Altiplano boasted the largest and richest city in the Americas, Potosí, founded beside a mountain of solid silver. But for the last two hundred years it has been an impoverished and backward region inhabited chiefly by pure-blooded Indians who survive on potatoes, almost the only crop the soil can produce, and on herds of llamas and alpacas. When the wealth of Potosí was exhausted, the Altiplano fell into oblivion, from which it has yet to rise.

Bolivia owns most of the Altiplano, though to the north the plain reaches into Peru, and to the south into Argentina. Almost all of the few travellers who venture south of La Paz, the modern capital of Bolivia, go as directly as possible to Chile or Argentina, because until they reach either they will be on the high plain, which has now acquired a reputation for utter emptiness. When writers do mention it they describe it as a hauntingly desolate land on which no one can live, baked by the sun in the day and frozen by every night of the year; the lonely landscape of a nightmare, whose hills, where there are hills, roll empty to the horizon. But I came from the south, and instead of crossing the Altiplano in three days by train, like most travellers, I spent three months making my way to Peru.

I was eighteen. I had spent two months working on a cattle station on the pampas, near Buenos Aires, and had six months free before returning to England. I travelled half the length of the Andes: from northern Argentina to Ecuador, from the southern boundary to the northern of the old Inca Empire. But most of my time was spent in reaching Cuzco, the capital and centre of the former Empire; on my way there I was able to fulfil my determination to see people who led lives entirely unlike mine. Though I had no idea what they were like, I wanted to visit 'primitive people'; and I did. This book is about my journey among them.

1

PORTICO A
LOS ANDES

A SINGLE SPOT of light travels the whole length of
the carriage, slowly passing from black window to
black window: a house somewhere out in the night. Men and
women sprawl over the wooden slatted benches, their faces
yellow in the dimness. From the far end comes the screech of
an accordion distorted by a cassette player turned too loud. In
the confusion of continually being jolted awake out of a heavy,
sweaty, dreamless sleep, the train has become a vehicle on its
way to hell. I might have been sleeping and repeatedly breaking the surface of consciousness for a week. My chest hurts.
This is a freakishly long night.

Then the relief of dawn, and I remember I am travelling to
Jujuy. I have left the pampas behind me, am heading for the
dry mountains of the north.

Others wake. Two boys opposite doing their national service sit up, sniff hard, rub their cheeks, light cigarettes. One pulls out a large thermos flask with a spout. He fills the lid with translucent coffee, sips, passes to his friend, draws on his cigarette; refills and, leaning forwards elbows on knees, he holds the lid out to me and says, 'Por favor.'

'Muchas gracias.' Weak, very sweet coffee.

The friend has a slab of white cheese in his hand, and a slab of some green jelly-like substance on a sheet of paper in his lap. He cuts me a chunk of each. The cheese is salty; the other substance is like firm, granular jam. He calls it 'dulce,' and it is sweet. You eat them together. They're disgusting. It takes me ten minutes to get through a matchbox-sized piece of each. I try to wash out my mouth by drinking from my water bottle; which I then pass to the one who gave me coffee.

'Muchas gracias,' he nods. He hesitates, then wipes the top on his sleeve; he drinks and passes to his friend. While I realize I forgot to wipe before handing it on. He sends me a quick grin; but his eyes show nervous suspicion: maybe I take his wiping of the spout as an offence, because I didn't do it.

He unbuttons his khaki cuff and rolls up the sleeve. On his swarthy wrist is a digital watch. He turns it round so the dial is on the underside of his arm. He glances at me, suppressing a smile. Is he proud of the watch?

I am disappointed. I had thought from their smooth high cheeks that these two might be Indians, press-ganged from a mountain village for their eighteen months of national service. But even if they do have native blood in their veins they aren't what I'm looking for: they are more interested in the trappings of the western world than in any ancient culture to which they might be heirs. They have been generous not only because they are kind: also because they want to associate with me, a true member of the modern world. The boy's eyes have a nervous glint because he doesn't know if he has really made contact with me, if he is really like me, which he wants to be.

I was travelling towards Bolivia, and ultimately to Cuzco in southern Peru. On the way I wanted to get to the most isolated villages. I wanted to find people who didn't wear nylon clothes and American company caps and digital watches, people who had none of the trappings of the modern world, who still lived ancient lives in sympathy with their environment. I was going to the highlands because there I was most likely to find traditional Indians.

The two boys sat back in their seats and glanced at me from time to time. The western horizon was now crumpled by distant hills: as we rattled north we were brought closer and closer to the Andes, the spine of the South American continent.

I was in a garage forecourt beside the main road north. A few miles back the tarmac had ended: there wouldn't be any more asphalt from here until Cuzco: dust tracks the whole way. One mile back I had passed a large concrete pyramid rising above the trees that surrounded it. It was the Tropic of Capricorn monument. This was the first hour of my life spent in the tropics.

But it wasn't hot. All about rolled hills, and I was high enough among them to be above tropical heat, though the ground was dry and sand-coloured. Here and there stood giant candelabra cacti, looming over the tangled thorn-bushes and low, brittle trees.

I spread out my map on the top of an oil-drum: there was the main road, a red line snaking northwards to the Bolivian border. It would take me to the purple patch on the map that marked the Altiplano, the great plateau stretching all the way across Bolivia, but I saw that if I followed the road I would miss the southern end of the plain, the Atacama highlands. I was eager not to do this, both because these highlands were the most backward and remote in Argentina, and the only area still to have any pure-blooded Indian population, and because I wanted to visit as much of the Altiplano as I possibly could. I needed to go west into the mountains at once.

Over to the left of the reassuringly solid red road on the map, in the very centre, east-west, of the mountains, was one

7

little black dot. It marked a village called Susques. A faint dotted line connected it to the main road. But there was no other settlement within a hundred miles of it. Even though I would undoubtedly have to retrace my steps afterwards, I determined to get to Susques anyway.

An old blue Peugeot rumbled into the garage. Two young men stepped out. One called the pump attendant. The other looked at me briefly, then shouted: 'Where are you going? To the north?'

'Sí. Al norte.'

'Come on them. Get in.'

The exhaust-pipe wasn't where it should have been. It was propped in the middle of the car, one end resting on the dashboard, the other on the ledge under the rear window. We growled out on the gravel road. Soon we were hurtling along, the tyres angrily spitting stones out of their way. On the loose surface we seemed to slide rather than turn round every bend. I could hardly believe the driver had any control, and he was driving the roaring car as fast as it would go.

Over the next four months I would get used to the feel of a dirt track.

'Walk four kilometres along that track and you'll come to Purmamarca. Good luck. Adiós.' The Peugeot thundered away, on up the main road.

I walked down a small valley filled with eucalyptus and almond trees. Between the trees the bare sandy walls of the valley would show here and there, studded with simple cacti-like stakes. Then among the trees there were houses of adobe, mud brick, and I came into a small plaza with a church and whitewashed walls: the village of Purmamarca.

It was deserted. There was no one about at all. I took off my rucksack and sat in the shade against a wall of the square.

What should I do now? On my map the track out to Susques was marked as starting from Purmamarca. Assuming the map was accurate then I should simply wait here until a vehicle on its way to Susques passed through. But when might that be?

Even the main road north to Bolivia, that was granted a bold red line on the map, was no more than a dirt track. What might that faint dotted line to Susques represent? The key claimed it was an all-season unpaved vehicular track. But did that mean anyone ever used it?

It was already late afternoon. As the light began to fail, men in open shirts wandered into the plaza smoking cigarettes. They were coming back from the fields and orchards. A door in one of the houses was opened by a fat woman. She left it open and retreated indoors.

The men who passed gave me cursory glances: I was not extraordinary to the inhabitants of Purmamarca; they were familiar with modern people. They weren't Indians, for the aboriginal inhabitants of this valley disappeared more than five hundred years ago. Those were the Purumamarca, conquered, despite fierce resistance, by the Incas. A few of their old dwellings and corrals lay tumbled on the valley sides: heaps of stones, nothing more. But among the ruins a nineteenth-century British archaeologist found the bones of a llama's foot which had been pierced with a bronze arrowhead. He interpreted this as indication that the llama had died a painful ritual death, even though he found no other part of the animal, and as proof that the Purumamarca practised llama worship. (But he assumed that an arrow was shot through the foot, which was subsequently chopped off, while the llama was alive; whereas it might have been dead already; or a stray arrow may have happened to land in a corral quite by accident. Only in this century has archaeology become a cautious science.)

By now it was too late for me to do anything but find food and a place to pitch my tent. The valley was engulfed in shadow, and the sky was a luminescent sheet over the dark world. The evening star was hanging above a hill, like a lamp switched on. Night would soon arrive.

People went in and out of the door the fat woman had left open: she kept a shop. It was a small, unlit room crammed full of all kinds of goods: buckets, trousers, great sacks of flour and rice, shelf upon shelf of tins, cigarettes, petrol: it was a store general enough for the inhabitants of Purmamarca rarely if ever to have to shop elsewhere.

Two women with long plaits stood talking in hushed voices to the shopkeeper behind her counter by the door. All three fell silent as I paid for a tin of sardines and a packet of crackers. Then one of them asked me if I was staying in Purmamarca for the night.

'Sí,' I told them. 'In my tent. And then I'm going to Susques.'

'A Susques? Cómo?' How?

'Are there no trucks that go to Susques?'

The shopkeeper shrugged her shoulders. The women hesitated, and then one of them said, 'But of course. *Por supuesto*. There are trucks. Tomorrow morning he'll find one.'

'Bueno,' said the shopkeeper. 'Tomorrow, then,' and in easy, flowing movements of her thick arms she slapped first one elbow, then the other, and then clapped her hands together in a lazy Argentinian gesture meaning That's that.

I pitched tent a little way out of the village on a patch of hard, dry ground which bent most of the pegs double. But I was in the right place: nailed to the tree beside which I camped was a sign that said, 'Susques 150 km.'

A crash of thunder woke me in the middle of the night. For five minutes, while a brief storm raged over Purmamarca, I lay with my face in my folded sweater wondering whether I had any idea what it was I planned to do, whether it was even possible for me to go to a tiny, remote settlement in the middle of the Argentinian Andes.

In the morning the sun came flooding into the valley and dried the tent before I had even crawled out. After I had made tea on my kerosene stove, I packed everything away and sat against the tree to wait for a truck. If I did not have a lift by the afternoon I would walk back to the main road and continue directly northwards to Bolivia. But I was lucky. I had been waiting only five minutes when I heard the sound of an engine approaching. A lorry appeared among the trees of Purmamarca. I put out my arm. The truck clanked and hissed to a stop beside me.

'Where are you going?' the driver asked from his window. He was very dark, with black hair, but of European descent.

'Susques.'

'To Susques? Why?—Well, as you like. I'm going half the way. Climb in the back if you want to see the mountains. We're going up high.'

The back was empty. It was a ribbed steel tank coated in dust. On the floor the scattered remnants of its last load, fine gravel, danced to the jounces. For a while the track stayed in the bottom of a ravine whose opposite wall, on the other side of a stream, had been cut by many rivulets into a row of great organ pipes. Some of these had heads and shoulders and looked like giant church statuary, but all fired in red clay. Then we began to climb: bend after bend, we swung back and forth, scaling the hillsides, until the valley became a mere cleft far below. Enormous smooth slopes flowed down to it from either side and ended in sudden cliff edges below which hung pleated curtains of rock. As the air became thinner the few clouds turned into slight wisps in the sky. More and more mountains rose up, barren and desolate, heaving and rolling away into the distance. Here and there stood a sudden sharp ridge of rock on a brow, the dorsal plates of a petrified dinosaur.

Only two things grew on these vast moors, a small brittle shrub with barely any life in it—they were parched, skeletal, grey things—and a cactus, a thin pole the height of a man. These cacti stood all over the slopes like soldiers, a crop of dragon's teeth, or strange offspring of the sun: down beat the sun on to these high naked hills and up sprang the cacti. They seemed deceitful things, the snakes of the plant kingdom: friends of the same destructive sun that had burnt away all other vegetation.

By the afternoon we had climbed up to 14,000 feet. Since leaving Purmamarca there had been no sign at all of humanity. These giant hills were the Puna de Jujuy. Puna, not a

Spanish but an Andean word, means a high, barren waste-land. If one were to travel further west, towards the Pacific, the land would become even drier, and one would cross the Atacama Desert, the desert where it hasn't rained for over a century. Its last inhabitants, the Atacameños, all but vanished over five hundred years ago. One ethnologist believed that the Atacameños once held an empire almost as great as the Incas', until a natural disaster—probably a drought—destroyed them all. His evidence was flimsy, consisting of a handful of words found in Peru and Bolivia that were of Atacama origin. Today, anyway, there are no more than a few isolated settlements of Atacameños, some on the Puna, some in the desert.

In the afternoon we reached a junction. Another track came down from the hills. It was our turning, and after a few minutes our destination appeared: a mining camp. Three men stepped out of the front of a pick-up truck. 'Buenas,' they called to my driver, who was climbing from his cab.

'I have brought a friend,' he said.

'Who?'

I had just jumped from the back of the lorry. 'Hola, buenas tardes.' One of the men, in a white T-shirt and jeans, came up to shake my hand. 'Where are you going? What are you doing here?'

'I am going to Susques,' I said.

'You won't find transport today. Stay the night here. Come on, bring your bags. Tomorrow morning we'll take you to the road for Susques.'

Against the head of the valley stood a row of concrete huts. The man in the T-shirt led me up to them.

'We're an exploratory mine,' he said as he locked a padlock on the door of the room where he had left my bag. 'I'm the foreman.'

He was a small man, under thirty, with limp black hair that fell over his eyes when he moved his head too abruptly, and a long thin moustache. His eyes were narrow and glinted.

'Come on,' he said. 'I'll show you our mine.'

We walked down to his Toyota pick-up truck. One of the

workers, in a yellow T-shirt and baseball cap, climbed in with us. We drove up a rough track that scaled a wall of the valley.

'Where are you from?' the foreman asked, looking at me as he drove round a hairpin bend.

'England.'

'Ah, I speak English,' he said in Spanish. Then leaning close to emphasize his words, 'Jou . . . peaky . . . panny. Jou peaky panny,' and he burst out laughing, glancing across me at his worker, who laughed too. We were skirting a drop of several hundred feet.

'Yes,' I said in English, 'I speak Spanish.'

'I . . . peaky Ingliss,' he laughed raucously. 'You must teach me more,' he added in his own tongue.

We stopped on a space levelled out on the shoulder of a hillside. The entrance to the mine, like a small cave-mouth, was set in a rockface. A ladder led down into the darkness. The foreman went first with his torch, the only light. The shaft was over a hundred feet deep. At the bottom there was as yet no more than a short tunnel too low to stand up in, with a pair of uneven rails running along its floor. The foreman shone his torch and took me stooping to the face at the end of the tunnel. He kicked at the loose rock with his boot: 'We are looking for nitrates,' he said. 'But we have a long way to dig. Deeper, deeper.'

On the way back up the ladder, which also served as rails for the wheeled buckets in which the excavations were hauled out, the altitude caught up with me. The foreman had told me that the mine was at 4800 metres, and whether it was the mere knowledge of that or the exertion of climbing in thin air, suddenly as I was nearing the top of the ladder I found I had broken out in a cold sweat and wanted to be sick. But the foreman was directly beneath me, so all I could do was cling to the ladder until the nausea and faintness subsided.

As soon as I reached the open air another wave of dizziness overcame me. My head filled with light. I heard the foreman cry out, and the ground swung up to hit the side of my head.

When I came to, the foreman and his worker were lifting

me out of the truck, chuckling to one another. They led me, arms slung round their necks, to a bed in one of their concrete huts. The foreman took a little glass vial from a box in a cupboard and emptied it into a tin cup of water. 'Drink this and sleep,' he said to me. 'It's good for *el soroche*. I'll wake you for supper.' I drained the cup, put my head down on the pillow, heard the foreman shut the door, and fell asleep.

The dozen miners ate supper round a big table in one of the huts. The room was dimly lit by gas-lamps, which though very bright to look at radiated no more than a weak glow around the room. All the men had had showers and combed their hair flat on their skulls. Most wore clean tracksuit tops and their best jeans with pressed creases. They were European Argentinians, with families down in the towns to the east of the Andes.

I had recovered completely. Over the meal the men grinned at me while the conversation turned about women and paternity. One man giggled and said, 'Me, I've got twenty sons.' Another asked me, 'How many have you got?'

'None,' I said innocently.

'How many women? He'—pointing to the foreman—'has got six women,' the man laughed.

The foreman smiled; and said in English: 'Jou, jou . . . how much, how much . . . geerls?' He laughed. 'Me—six.'

'And how many sons?' I asked.

'Thirty, maybe thirty-five . . . I don't know.' At this everyone roared with laughter.

Later the foreman told me what he knew about the area. 'A few years ago a cadaver was found nearby, at Salinas Grandes. You'll go there tomorrow on the way to Susques. It was an ancient person, a thousand or two thousand years old, dressed in brilliant textiles which were preserved perfectly. Perfectly. Why? Because the person had been buried in a saltlake—which you'll see tomorrow.'

'Who was it?'

'It was an Atacameño. A man. He was sitting with his chin

14

on his knees, in the posture of the Indian dead. There used to be plenty of Indians here, so they say. They say the climate has changed—it used to be fertile. Still, there are a few Indians left. Most of the inhabitants of Susques are Atacameños. It's one of their last communities. None of them speak Spanish there. But they won't stay that way much longer. A road is being built to Chile from Susques. They'll have trucks coming through within a couple of years. Our lorries will use the road to reach the Pacific ports . . . If we ever find any nitrate.'

It was still dark, and astonishingly cold. I had been left here at a crossroads by the man from the mining camp. The foreman had told me I would soon get a lift to Susques. It was very early. As the growl of the truck became inaudible its two yellow rear lights, like a pair of eyes, showed up a fog of dust in its trail.

Dawn came fast. First the air became pale blue. This was enough to reveal that I was in a wide saucer in the mountains, and that the floor of it was a saltlake: a sickly white presence glowing strangely in the earliest twilight. Then the mountains behind were welded into one single flat dark purple silhouette with a keen, jagged edge catching brilliant light. This blade grew ever sharper and brighter: the sun was climbing up towards its edge unseen. Meanwhile away over on the far side of the white sheet of salt the mountains were a long, low jumble of blue humps on which red and pink faces had been scratched. The air, all murkiness dispelled, was thin and clear now.

Tentatively I walked out on to the salt, the quiet crunch of my feet, as on packed snow, the only sound. Away stretched the flat white expanse, to the pink mountains on the far side, now blue at their bases. It was unearthly, the bed of an evaporated prehistoric sea. So strong is the sun at this high altitude that it has burnt lakes away. The Atacameño who was found in this saltlake might in fact have drowned in an inland sea now evaporated, and sunk into its sediment. Around this white sheet the mountains were comforting and homely.

Already a small patch of sky above the near ridge was too bright to look at. Suddenly, without my noticing, the tip of the sun appeared, and very soon the whole saltlake was dazzling white. As the sun freed itself from the ride and rose higher the liquid clarity of the air evaporated with the dew, and a heavy, oppressive heat at once set in.

It was to be a long day. The mine's foreman had driven me down here because there was a junction, which ought to have doubled my chances of a lift on to Susques. He thought the other track was very busy, especially early in the morning. But it was hard to believe: the track was nothing more than the wheel-marks in the dust of several lorries passing the same way.

The saltlake was like a frozen virgin snowfield. In the distance the white gave in to mirages, long bands of blue and grey that shifted and quivered and vanished suddenly if you sat down, to reappear nearer on the lake. It was confusing to the eye, for some of these watery strips looked so much like the sky that the mountains beyond seemed to be airborne, like a fleet of solidified clouds.

I walked back to the crossroads, already feeling the heat of the sun, and sat down on my bag to wait for a lift. There was not the slightest breath of wind, nor any sound. The sun beat down on to the salt. The foreman had said I would get a lift within an hour or two; an hour at least had already passed. The sun was well up in the sky now, and I had neither seen nor heard any sign of a vehicle coming. A dull anxiety began to grow in me, sitting in this strange, desolate place beside the saltlake, as smooth as a lake and as hostile as a desert. I tried to read, but the thought of being stuck here in such a remote, barren valley was too distracting. I had enough water for a day or two, and the miners had given me a bag of crackers and apples. Their camp was probably no more than a day's walk away. But here I was, waiting and waiting in hope that a lorry might pass. It was impossible to do anything but look around, vainly scanning the hills for a cloud of dust, and automatically throw stones at the small tufts of straw that grew here and there.

If I didn't get a lift today, what would I do? How long would I wait? Would my sleeping-bag be warm enough for the fierce cold of a night out here? Would I die of hypothermia? And what if nothing came tomorrow either?

I saw something moving. It was far over on the other side of the saltlake: among the shivering bands of mirage there were two black ants, one under the other, slowly moving to the left. It was a strain to see them. Maybe the track skirted the saltlake. Maybe it was a lorry on its way round to me. The dots stopped. Then they moved slowly along to the right. Had they dropped something? Then they were moving to the left again; then back to the right. They were to travel their short course back and forth for the rest of the day.

There was little to interrupt the monotony of anxiety. I saw a small yellow bird fluttering among the shrubs. So I was not the only living thing here. When the bird saw me it flew away.

Later on, I imagined I heard the sound of an engine a great distance away. Straining my ear I could hear it distinctly: a low, steady purr. I scoured the hills all around for a trace of a dust-cloud: none: all was still. But the sound became clearer and stronger. So was it real or imagined? I listened more intently, and the growl grew still louder; but it seemed too low and steady for a lorry. By now it was quite distinct, and familiar. Suddenly I realized what it was. My attentiveness collapsed, the alertness of my senses dropped: it was just an aeroplane.

When the sun was overhead another bug appeared on one of the tracks. I watched it grow. There was no noise. It became a stick, walking oddly. It became a man in a hat. But he was strange. His head didn't move at all, yet his feet trod heavily down and up. And his belt flashed. He was wearing black. Sometimes his feet flashed. He was only a hundred yards away when I realized he was on a bicycle.

The man wound up to me and jumped off his machine to tug it to a stop. 'Buenos días, señor,' he exclaimed. He was panting. He wore a dark suit with a white shirt and a sweater under his jacket. The leathery skin of his face was stretched tight over his cheekbones. 'What are you doing here?'

'I'm going to Susques.'

'How? On foot?'

'I'm waiting for a lorry.'

'Ah,' he said, and nodded as if he had just discovered I had a private arrangement for travel. 'I know some days there are trucks that pass.' With that he was off, lurching along with his bicycle until it was rolling fast enough to balance when he jumped on.

The afternoon dragged by. The air was still and hot. I ate some crackers, and wished that I had more water. I lay down on the dusty, stony earth, trying to doze. I tried to read again, but could not concentrate.

When the sun was well across the saltlake, hanging above the mountains on the far side, I began to think about where I would pitch my tent. I would have to kick and sweep clear of stones a patch of ground. Or perhaps I would use the track itself.

A whole day had passed. One snowy peak in the distance gathered clouds around itself as the sun was beginning to descend. It made me think of the Alps with their huge blue shadows as night draws in; and then I looked round and saw the saltlake glinting beneath the sun.

All about the mountains stood desolate. As my eye wandered aimlessly over them one more time, for lack of anything else to do, I noticed, wavering in the heat, far up the track I had come down before dawn, something against a hillside that could have been dust in the air. I stared and stared, and there definitely was a little column of dust hovering there. A tiny black dot appeared at the foot of it. I went out on the track. It was long and straight coming off the lower slopes of the hills, and I could hear nothing. The column of dust was barely moving, but the dot beneath it grew, and became a little beetle, and now even glinted at me. It became a shaking toy truck. Desperately I ran back to pack my things away and then stood in the middle of the track, my bag at my feet. At last an engine became audible. The truck continued to grow and shake. Now it was only a few hundred yards away. I could see its radiator grinning at me. Suddenly I was worried it might not stop. I waved my arm, then both my arms. Its headlights flashed. What did that mean? Get out of the way? I could hear the engine clearly, and it had not dropped in pitch.

Not until the pick-up truck was standing beside me did I realize that it was indeed going to stop. It was small and red and laden with boxes and crates behind the cab. I walked to the window.

'Muchas gracias, muchas gracias,' I said to the driver.

'De nada.' He, like the man with him, wore sunglasses, a moustache and a tracksuit top. 'Well,' he said, 'where do you want to go?' He did not smile.

'Susques.'

'Susques? Why?—All right, climb in. Put your bag in the back. You are lucky. We're going to Susques. But quick. We must get there in time for supper. They'll be getting hungry. We're bringing the food.'

The track to Susques went straight across the saltlake. From inside a truck, knowing I was on my way to a village, it was no longer frightening. The smooth crust hummed and hissed as the tyres raced over it. The mountains had become great brown masses floating above a pale blue mirage that shimmered all around the shore.

The driver turned to me and spoke across his companion: 'We're building a road.'

'You're the roadbuilders,' I said.

'You knew about the road?'

'I was told.'

'All the way to Chile. A hundred and thirty-five kilometres. I'm the foreman. Antonio.'

I nodded to him.

'And this is Juan Miguel.'

I shook his companion's hand. He smiled at me, showing dirty teeth.

19

'What is your name?' he asked, his voice deep and gravelly.

'Enrique.'

Antonio repeated, 'Enrique. Bueno. And where are you from?'

'England.'

'What are you doing here? Why do you want to go to Susques?'

'I hope to see Atacameño Indians.'

'Ah. Sí, sí. The Susqueños are Indians. *Gente antigua.*' Ancient people.

Juan Miguel pulled a plastic bag of coca leaves out of his trouser pocket. He gave me a little wad and showed me where to put it, between teeth and cheek on one side. They were dry and brittle. They cracked if squeezed between finger and thumb. They softened after a few minutes in my mouth, and I began to taste them: bitter like spinach; but they also numbed my tongue and gums.

'Good for the journey,' said Juan Miguel. 'Hunger and thirst and tiredness disappear.'

We crossed the salt and picked up the track again on the far side. Along a narrow defile of bright red rock; then up on to the shoulders of hills, climbing towards an enormous ridge like the keel of a capsized hull. As we made the brow itself suddenly a vast plain came into view below, a land criss-crossed by deep gorges, reaching far into a blue haze. It was a huge landscape. In the thin, high air the plain could be seen stretching northwards for hundreds of miles. My sense of scale was upset. For a moment I thought I was looking at a greatly magnified image of skin.

'El Altiplano,' said Antonio. He waved his hand towards the plain and said, 'All the way to Bolivia then all the way to Peru.'

It seemed impossible that this vast highland could be inhabited. It was like coming upon an enormous unknown plateau. I couldn't believe that I would be able to travel across it.

We wound in and out of two more gulleys, and then dropped into a deep gorge flaming orange in the sun's last glare. At the bottom was a brown ribbon of water flanked by threadbare strips of green. We rounded a corner high up on the canyon wall and there below, huddled between the little river and the opposite wall, was Susques.

'Not very big,' said Antonio. It was a cluster of earthen houses with tin roofs. 'Just a little village.'

But it was an amazing sight: a settlement at last. It was like reaching a promised land: a river, vegetation, however scanty, and houses, and all in this desolate, empty land where no one else lived. On a hillside above the little clustered village chalk stones had been laid out to form giant letters. They must have been for passing aeroplanes to see. Even though they were in the heart of the mountains the words they spelt were: 'Susques—Portico A Los Andes'.

We forded the brown river and entered the village—red adobe homes glowing in the dusk. The roadbuilders used a large one-room house as their dining hall. When we drew up outside it three men came out to greet their foreman and help unload the provisions. Antonio introduced me and told them I would be staying with them. Like the miners, they were modern Argentinians living here in temporary exile for their work. They grinned and laughed when they heard I was from England, welcoming a visitor from the civilized world.

When the provisions were unloaded Antonio offered to show me Susques. It was twilight now among the houses. Each one had a glass window set in its clay wall, and an open doorway. Most of the inhabitants seemed to be out in the street, or standing in front of their doors in pairs. There were small groups at every corner. All of them had swarthy faces, which were turned towards us, and bright black eyes. Many seemed to breathe through their mouths only, and kept their lips open showing their teeth in an expression like a grin. All of them had the high, prominent cheekbones of Indians.

They were wearing strange combinations of western clothes: old tracksuits, dark suits from the 1940s, dirty broad-checked chefs' trousers. One grinned at me from under a big Stetson. Their clothes were all scruffy and dusty, and didn't seem to suit them, as if the people had been strapped into their gear unwillingly, like children.

They stared at us as we walked by. Whenever I looked at them they would turn away shyly; then glance back over their shoulders to see if I was still looking. Sometimes they would retreat giggling behind the corner of a street or into a doorway and shut the door. The door would creak open slowly and slam shut again if I was still facing it. Yet when my back was turned they couldn't take their eyes off me and my funny clothes, as if they had heard about foreigners but never or seldom seen one.

'Who are these people?' I asked Antonio.

'They're Puneños, no more,' he replied. 'They're just Atacameños.'

Western influence had clearly reached this little village. But as yet it didn't seem to have altered the mentality of the people. They were fascinated by me, a creature from the modern world; but they were also nervous, and behaved ingenuously, as if they felt they need have no dignity in front of me because I was so different; as if I did not belong in their conception of humanity.

On one side of the village, enclosed in an adobe wall, was a sixteenth-century Dominican church. It only served to reinforce the impression of childish ingenuousness that the Susqueños gave. Four hundred years ago they had allowed foreigners to invade the village, and to build a peculiar house in which no one would live; and still they let it stand. Surely they weren't Christians? Or perhaps they were: perhaps they had acquiesced to performing strange rites on which the foreigners insisted. Perhaps they had accepted the Catholic faith dumbly, as they had assumed western dress.

The strangest thing was that they should have adopted these things from outside apparently without being changed by them. They looked at me as children might do at an elephant, with wide-eyed wonder and fear, from the safety of their doorways. They saw no connection between their church and clothes and me. Even though another culture had reached them, they were innocent, still, of the rest of the world. They were unaware that they were Indians.

The Dominican Fathers travelled over much of the fallen Inca Empire within the first four decades after the Spaniards reached Peru. They baptized thousands of natives and built churches along the way. In exchange for these services they exacted tributes which were deemed so heavy even by the Spanish authorities that by 1577 they had been expelled from all the New Provinces of Spain. So Susques experienced no more than a few years of Dominican zeal. For the last four centuries Susques had probably been left largely undisturbed, so remote and small and insignificant a settlement was it. Yet the church was still standing, roofed and swept within and evidently whitewashed on its front wall within the last few years. Did someone usher the Susqueños into church once a week?

'Sí,' Antonio told me over supper. 'Each month a priest comes from Purmamarca. Second Sunday of the month.'

'Are they really Christians, then?' I asked.

Antonio was chewing a mouthful of corned beef fritter. He swallowed and wiped his black moustache with the side of a finger. 'Of course. All Argentina is Catholic. Except perhaps for parts of Patagonia.'

The cook, a meticulous man with Indian-looking cheeks, had made a paste of mashed corned beef and chopped onion. He was standing at a sideboard next to the stove. Slowly and regularly he made pats of the mush, dipped them in a bowl of whisked egg, then patted them in a plate of flour, and laid them sizzling in a pan of oil. Every few minutes he would take a bowl from the dining table, refill it with his fritters, and put it back. His expression, a faint smile of satisfaction in his own competence, never changed.

'So are there no indigenous religions in Argentina?' I asked.

'Religions, no,' said Antonio, sticking his fork into the fritter bowl. 'But there are superstitions, as you find all over the world.'

'Do they have any here?'

'I don't know. I'm only here to work. But probably.' He shrugged his shoulders and carried on eating.

After supper the workers brought out an instruction booklet for a bulldozer. The instructions appeared in Japanese, English, German, Swedish and Turkish, but not in Spanish. They had had the bulldozer for over a month and hadn't yet managed or dared to start it up. They wanted me to translate the whole thing for them, and sat around eagerly waiting for me to explain what all the diagrams meant and what all the levers in the pictures were. But my Spanish didn't extend to technical names. I didn't even know the Spanish for a clutch, I now realized. So I tried to describe the functions of the items shown in the first figure. The workers would all nod vigorously and chorus, 'Sí, sí,' when they thought they understood my garbled phrases. But they were jumping to conclusions I hadn't intended. I kept shaking my head and saying, 'No sé, no sé.' I don't know. Antonio finally realized that I could not help and put the booklet away.

He smiled at me. *'Es difícil.* We'll have to wait for the new book to arrive. But it doesn't matter. For the moment we can carry on with our truck and our shovels.'

It would be longer than the miners expected before their nitrates were travelling down to Pacific ports.

By nine-thirty the roadbuilders had all gone off to their quarters, leaving me to sleep on the floor of their dining hall. I climbed into my sleeping-bag and pulled its mouth tight around my neck, against the cold of an Andean night, and felt satisfied, even excited, by what I regarded as an accomplishment. I had made it to Susques, and I was about to sleep among the homes of the last Atacameño Indians.

The morning was icy. I had slept fitfully on the earth floor. I heard the cook putting water on to boil while it was still dark, but I had such a searing headache that I couldn't bring myself to get up. Some of the workers came in. They were standing against the wall waiting for me to clear the floor so they could take the chairs off the table. In a daze, aware of little but the effects of altitude, I picked myself up. It was only when seated at the table as I rested my cheek on my hand that I discovered how badly my face was sunburnt from the previous day by the saltlake.

One of the roadworkers was driving a lorry to Purmamarca that day. 'I don't know,' said Antonio, 'but there may not be anyone else leaving here for another two or three weeks. If you don't want to stay till then you'd better go with him.' So after coffee and bread I set off.

I lay in the back, on the lorry's load of earth. Decent soil was evidently a commodity worth transporting. It had fallen into a comfortable slope; I could lie back and see everything around me. Each day in the Andes is said to contain all four seasons of the year. Now it was still winter, and I wasn't wearing enough clothes. But as the lorry pulled away, crossed the river and started climbing up the side of the gorge, the shadows peeled back and the sun reached me. The hills were still wet with dew and glistened; but spring was coming on. My headache subsided.

All day I made my way, with a series of lifts, up the Quebrada de Humahuaca. This canyon leads up on to the Altiplano like a ramp cut into the side of the Andes. I had decided to make directly for Bolivia now. There I hoped to visit strings of villages at least as remote as Susques, and perhaps free of all western influence. Over the next four months I would never be lower than twelve thousand feet.

It was in the back of a priest's truck with three Indian women that I finally rolled into La Quiaca, the frontier town. The women, each with two long black plaits and a derby hat, swayed back and forth silently to the bends. Each had several bundles tied up in colourful blankets under her legs, in her lap, on her back. They looked at me with disapproving sneers, as if I were doing something wrong. Or perhaps they didn't like the Padre's driving; they muttered whenever a tight bend sent their bundles rolling across the floor.

The sun went down, abandoning the bleak hills to the cold.

25

The Indian women wrapped themselves in blankets. I crossed my arms and leaned on my knees. Freezing night fell.

Next day I crossed into Bolivia. La Quiaca is but one half of a town; the other half is called Villazón and is in Bolivia, on the far side of a small ravine which marks the border. There used to be a cage on wires which spanned the frontier, but a bridge has been built now.

In La Quiaca the streets were paved and pedestrians walked on the swept pavements. Every shopkeeper had a broom for keeping his section of the pavement clean. Villazón was different. The streets were plain earth and were filled with the bright colours of Indian clothes. Everywhere people were sitting out in the street; there were people selling *empanadas*, little pastries, from big baskets, *helados*, ice creams that were really mousses, and warm, from big trays, oranges from sacks, pieces of grilled meat fished out of wide enamel bowls and wrapped in brown paper. It was like coming from a school playground during lessons to one during a break. And everywhere Indian women, with their derby hats and bowler hats, their blazingly colourful cardigans and skirts, shuffling about with things folded up in their striped blankets; and everywhere people climbing into the wooden backs of lorries like cattle-holds, swinging up endless sackfuls and blanketfuls of belongings, putting dust into the air which drifted in clouds out of the shadows of the trucks into the sunlight, which turned it into golden smoke.

I was in a different country.

2

SALTLAKE

MOST of the Indians of the Bolivian Altiplano are Aymaras. No one knows how long they have been here; only that like all the aboriginal inhabitants of the New World they came down from the Bering Strait within the last fifty thousand years, and are unlikely to have reached the central Andes earlier than fifteen thousand years ago.

For most of the first millennium AD the Aymaras held an empire centred on the site of the temples of Tiahuanaco. Their influence, if not their dominion, spread wide in the Andes. The motifs of their religious symbolism have been found as far afield as northern Peru and Chile. Even the Incas' empire was hardly wider. But by 1000 AD the Aymaras had disintegrated into twelve small, mutually hostile kingdoms, all of them on the Altiplano. By 1500 AD these had been fully incorporated in the Inca Empire. But it wasn't then that Aymara

27

life changed dramatically; it was in the late sixteenth century, when Viceroy Toledo of Upper Peru (as the Spaniards called the Altiplano) instituted his reforms.

Toledo attempted to reduce the number of Indian settlements by creating towns for surrounding villagers to move into. Each town had a plaza; and with the introduction of the western week with its one free day in every seven—an incredible frequency for the Indians—the conditions were perfect for the growth of markets. There was a regular day for it, and a regular place for it, the local town plaza. Andean people, whose local crops are closely determined by the altitude at which their fields happen to be, had always needed to exchange produce with one another. But as the weekly markets became common, exchange grew into more than the provision of basic needs. There emerged a class of Indians, Cholos, who made marketing their main economic activity. Their numbers swelled until they became the most conspicuous Indians on the Altiplano, and ubiquitous. Only the most remote Aymaras continued their traditional lives. The rest became Cholos.

Today most of the Indians you see in Bolivia are Cholos. They have a distinctive dress: the women wear bowlers or derby hats, colourful skirts and cardigans, and many layers of petticoats; the men wear suits, generally old and tatty ones. Most of the Altiplano's townspeople are Cholos. They have adopted Spanish as their *lingua franca,* but many Cholos can still speak their native Aymara dialects, and some maintain Aymara customs. They are a class, not a tribe: they are Aymaras who have abandoned agricultural life and taken to the towns.

In fact, many a Cholo household is divided down the middle. While the husband cultivates fields, his wife may spend most of her active life selling his harvest along with any other goods she can lay hold of. For it is the Cholo women who are the marketers, who generate the funds in a Cholo family. Cholo men often seem listless and ineffectual. Sometimes at markets they help their wives by carrying sacks of vegetables around; some have crops to tend; others are artisans. But none make money like their wives. It is only at fiestas, where money is spent, that Cholo men come into their own.

Uyuni is a bleak desert town. Its wide, dusty streets lead on to a windswept plain. It is cold, and its square buildings are all pale shades of grey. It lies, like a dismal fungus on the plain, a few miles from the vast Salar de Uyuni, the biggest saltlake in America.

I reached Uyuni at midnight. It was bitterly cold. Only five other passengers left the train here. The rest would be going on to Oruro. We were escorted out of the station and across a wide open street by three soldiers: since the last coup d'état a few months ago there had been a curfew in operation. The soldiers took us straight to the nearest hotel, where a small old man in a suit and panama hat appeared from behind a high counter carrying a kerosene lamp that hissed and made the folded skin of his cheeks yellow. He led the others off through a doorway, then came back to guide me, without a word, but breathing noisily, along a corridor, across a yard, and into a cramped room with three low-slung beds. I saw by his weak light that two of the beds were occupied.

I would have protested and asked for a single room, but I was tired and the cold was too fierce for a discussion. He went away, leaving me to undress in the dark.

In the morning I was woken by a dialogue between the occupants of the two beds either side of mine. The voices were hoarse, male and spoke in lazy drawls.

'Cuántas?' How many?

'No sé.'

'Diez o doce por lo menos.' At least ten or twelve.

'Más, más.' More, more.

I opened my eyes and looked cautiously either way. Both speakers were huddled under coarse grey blankets with their heads hidden.

'Don Hilario, hoy es sabado. Esta noche vamos a beber unas veinte cervezas más.' A gruff laugh followed, which became a

29

hacking cough that was finally silenced by the sound of a match striking.

'Francisco, are we late?'

'Of course.'

'Have classes already begun?' The smell of tobacco reached my nostrils.

'Half an hour ago. Maybe we should take the day off, Don Hilario. It's only a half day.'

'But who will teach them?'

'No one, as usual.'

This seemed to serve by mutual consent as a cue for both speakers to climb out of bed. They must have been sleeping in their clothes, for I heard no dressing, and there was too little time for it anyway before one of them saw me and said: 'Excuse us, señor. This is a great surprise—Muy buenos días.'

I stopped pretending to be asleep, and opened my eyes on two lanky young men with mops of black hair and keen black eyes. Both were dressed in dusty nylon cardigans and slacks. One had a modest straight nose and a broad prominent brow-ridge spread above his smooth cheeks, while the other had a long thin beak that curved round towards his lips, and close-set eyes.

'Buenos días,' I said. My clothes were within reach on the floor, having begun the night folded under my head as a pillow until I had found that the bed sagged as much as a hammock and had brushed them away. I began the operation of dressing in bed.

'Please excuse us for waking you,' said the long-nosed one, simpering.

I apologized for intruding on them.

'Not at all,' he said. 'I see that you are not Bolivian. We are honoured—May I introduce myself? Don Hilario Fonseca Chávez.' He nodded slowly.

'And Don Francisco Nuñez,' said the other.

The sheets had wrapped themselves around my legs while I was tussling with my trousers. Once I had wrested myself free I stood to shake their hands. 'Enrique.' They smiled and nodded repeatedly. I added, 'From England.'

'Qué bueno,' said Don Hilario.

I noticed now that two tatty tartan overnight bags stood on the floor on either side of the door, and beside each was a stack of school textbooks. 'You are schoolteachers.'

'Sí, sí. We have been here for six months trying to educate the young Uyuneños. *Muy difícil.* They are very different from the people of La Paz.'

Don Francisco smiled at me. 'Sadly we are in a great hurry now. We must leave at once.' He held his hands together in front of his chest as if about to bow like a Chinaman. 'Please excuse us.'

'Of course.'

'Until later, then.'

'Hasta luego,' echoed Don Hilario. And they disappeared.

No one else was up in the hotel. In the courtyard, whose adobe walls were set with the eight wooden doors of the hotel's rooms, three thin hens with bald necks were pecking at the dirt. They crooned and muttered quietly.

I walked out of the hotel to stroll around Uyuni, and to find some breakfast. The streets were enormous wide avenues, empty of vegetation, planted with street-lamps. Men in black suits stood in scattered groups along the broad roads. They made the town seem a ghost town, as if these few inhabitants were the last remnants of a population that had been, and were dwarfed by the size of their settlement. Each street ended abruptly, simply stopped and the land was there reaching away, flat and empty. For this was the real Altiplano, a vast flatland, a tableland trestled by the two Cordilleras of the Andes. Uyuni was no more than a little blemish on its emptiness.

On one street stood a large concrete hall. A woman sat next to its open doorway with two small pyramids of oranges on a sheet beside her. High above, the words *Mercado Municipal* had been painted in red on the wall. I went in.

It was twilight inside. Pillars of concrete rose up to the roof in two rows. Beneath them the hall had been divided into rows of concrete stalls, each with a counter in front and a shelf behind. Between them sat Chola women, their bowler hats and shaded faces visible above piles of dirty fruit and stacks of browning meat. Dressed like absurd travesties of circus clowns and silently chewing coca leaves with their mouths agape, the women were almost sinister: their enormously wide skirts which reached only to the knees, their outrageously bright shirts and cardigans, all a blaze of colours, and above them, barely noticeable, their dark faces; and perched on top the little bowler hats. It was all an extraordinary miscarriage of western dress. The hats were not in the least practical: they were not warm, they were always several sizes too small, and they weren't even intended for women. Though they were once obligatory, now they are worn only through habit. Yet they seem like a deliberate effort to dress up, to assert a cultural identity; even to mock the foreigners who introduced the hats in the first place.

Beneath these bowlers their faces, framed by long plaits of jet black hair, were witch-like. They were nearly attractive, for Indian women have high cheekbones which are often beautiful. But their faces narrow so abruptly from the middle of the cheeks to small, drawn mouths that they look misshapen. The women are invariably plump and waddle about in their puffed-out skirts; but their faces, however wide in the cheeks, are always drawn and wrinkled around the mouth. They rarely look at you; when they do it is grudgingly, the whites of their dark eyes flashing suspiciously for an instant, standing out sharply from the swarthiness of their skin.

The women who sold breakfast sat along the walls of the market: coffee, bread, hot milk. They were like the other women, among their huge aluminium saucepans. I went from one to the next asking for coffee. Either they would look aside and fix their eyes silently on the far wall or they would squeal: 'No hay. Ya no hay café.' There's no coffee left. 'No hay' was pronounced like an expression of pain. They wouldn't look at me, except fleetingly when I was about to move on.

They seemed all the more witch-like for their apparent resentment of my presence. They were all unfriendly, as if conspiring in some sinister plot. Two women revealed they did have coffee but asked absurdly high prices for it. It seemed they had an inborn resentment of Europeans, as if my visit to the market were a further violation of their ancient culture, as if I were prying into their lives. To give me breakfast, and at the right price, would be to give in, or to put themselves out far beyond the limits of pride.

Finally I did get breakfast. When I left the hall it felt as if the whole place was relieved, as if a rarely used muscle, unexpectedly tightened, could now relax.

Outside it was bright. The wide, dusty street stretched away to the plain in both directions. Instead of being filled with people, the streets of the town were still almost deserted. It was the wind that filled them, the bitterly cold wind coming off the plain.

Nearby there was another market, outdoors. Wooden stalls with corrugated iron roofs stood in rows. Some were shut up, closed to the cold wind, some open like late flowers that should long ago have withered and disappeared for winter. Between the rows there was no one. I walked down, past a few women who sat inside a stall among stacks of bright nylon clothes. I happened to glance into another open stall further on and noticed a pair of sunglasses I liked. I went in under the roof.

It was run by a middle-aged man. He wore a suit and a hat and an open skirt: he was a Cholo.

I picked up the sunglasses. The lenses were made of heavy green glass. The frame was chipped, so they obviously weren't new. I said, 'How much?'

'Cien pesos,' the man answered firmly. That was four dollars.

'Es mucho, no?'

'Then have one of these,' he pointed to a rack of brand new sunglasses.

They were all made of light plastic. I liked the weight of the old pair.

'These are all fifty,' said the man. 'Very cheap, no?'

33

I held up the old pair and showed him where they were damaged. 'How can they be twice the price of the new ones?'

He took them from my hand with a little smile and put them in his jacket pocket.

'Señor,' I said, 'but I want to buy them.'

'They're not for sale,' he grinned. 'Too old.'

My haggling had gone all wrong. 'Por favor, señor, por favor.'

He shook his head, smiling. He was enjoying this; I was getting exasperated. I pleaded and pleaded, my heart increasingly set on that old pair.

Finally he leaned down underneath his counter and drew out a sheet of paper. 'Where are you from? Norte America?'

'No, Inglaterra.'

'Bueno, write me down some English phrases.'

'What?'

'Buenas tardes, buenos días, muchas gracias, por favor—in English. Write me down. Here.' He gave me a pen.

'Why?' I asked, perplexed. 'Can I buy the glasses after?'

'We'll see.'

When I had written out five phrases he studied the sheet closely, then reached under the counter again to bring out an old typewriter. 'Type them out for me,' he said. All this was done with an amused grin. He was having a good joke seeing how far he could push the bargaining process, and me.

I typed out the words, and their translations; and asked if the glasses were for sale again. He examined the paper—and said no. So I snatched it from his hand and threatened to be off with it. He begged me to give it back, smirking; but I wouldn't. So he took the sunglasses from his pocket and set them on the wooden counter. 'And how much?' I asked, still holding the paper out of his reach.

'Setenta pesetas, no más,' he said with an apologetic frown: seventy little pesos, no more.

I gave him the money and the paper. He nodded with satisfaction and smiled at me, holding out his hand. I was still confused, but shook his hand anyway, and smiled back.

By the afternoon the male inhabitants of Uyuni, the strag-
glers who hadn't left the town yet, were all blind drunk. It was
Saturday and there was even less to do than on other days. It
was time for the week to become interesting. Instead of standing motionless along the walls of the streets the sparse clusters of men staggered out into the middle and accosted one
another or exchanged drinks of pure sugar alcohol and beer.

I met the two schoolteachers back in the hotel room, and
told them that I was keen to see traditional peoples. I obviously had to leave the railway line. Uyuni had a population
that seemed to suffer the same effects of modern influence as
the Eskimos and Aborigines: listlessness and alcoholism. It
was clear I had to get to more remote villages if I were to see
unspoilt Andean life.

'You must go across the *salar*,' Don Hilario told me, 'All
around the Salar de Uyuni there are *gente antigua*.'

'But how do I get there?'

'You have to go by truck. Go to the Lorry Drivers' Syndicate.'

I found the Lorry Drivers' Syndicate in a row of concrete
bungalows. I needed to travel west from here, out on to the
great saltlake, and in Bolivia lorries serve as buses. Although
the lorries are slow, uncomfortable and unsheltered, for me
they had only advantages: you could see everything you
passed, since the lorries had open holds contained by chest-
high walls; you had ample time to observe, because the lorries
were so slow; and you couldn't feel stuffy or sick.

The man in the Lorry Drivers' Syndicate, who smiled cu-
riously throughout my enquiry, wondering why anyone, let
alone a westerner, should want to go to such backward places,
took me outside and pointed out with flat movements of his
palm the route to where the lorry for Llica left. Llica was a
town very near Chile, on the other side of the Salar de Uyuni.
The lorry left on Sunday morning, the next day.

That night I decided to have a beer. Now that the altitude
no longer gave me hangovers I recklessly sought an artificial
one. In the first bar that I went to, a dimly lit place with a

wooden counter and wooden tables, I saw the two school-teachers sitting in a corner. They waved me over, and before I noticed they had ordered three more beers. Beers only came in litre bottles. I was pouring out my first glassful from the new bottle when three more arrived. The schoolteachers' faces shone. Everything began to glisten and glow and I felt so good, caution already drowned, that it seemed natural to follow glassful with glassful and to agree with the teachers that all men are brothers, including the Germans who set up the brewery in the capital of Bolivia.

Then we were outside, immune to the bitter cold of the night. Then in a long upstairs room eating steak and chips. It was llama meat, delicious and salty. The chips were also salty, the best I ever ate. We needed more beer to wash it all down.

Next thing, I was balancing on the plank on which you had to crouch to use the lavatory in the hotel. Beneath was a pit which buzzed with flies during the day. It was pitch black in the hut, a blackness thick with odour. The world began to spin, exerting a powerful centrifugal force on my head. With a supreme effort of will I abandoned my attempt; and woke to a shocking morning, on my bed.

That morning I went along past the outdoor market to where the lorry for Llica left. It was parked in the middle of a wide street. People were already climbing up the small ladder into the back and passing their bundles and blankets up.

'Is this lorry going to Llica?' I asked an old man. He was wearing a dirty black suit and carrying two heavy bundles wrapped up in blankets with stripes of violently bright colours.

'Yes. To Llica. I'm going to Llica,' he replied.

I climbed in and sat down in a corner at the back. There were people sitting all over the floor of the lorry, except at the back. Some old men were putting sacks up on a shelf above the cabin, all wearing dark tatty suits and woollen hats. The women, as colourful as the blankets, complained and whined about things getting damaged. More and more people climbed in, until the entire volume of the hold was filled with humanity. There were even two men holding on outside.

A woman was sitting at the edge of the road with a bag of small loaves of bread beside her, saying, 'Pan, pan,' intermittently in a thin, high voice and looking down the street distractedly. There was a boy selling ice creams from a big tray. He walked round the lorry shouting, 'Helados, helados,' speeding up with each repetition so it sounded like, 'Eladdoss, elats, lats,' his young tongue skipping through the consonants.

In the bland, dusty street the lorry was the focus of everyone's attention. It was a small splash of colour between the pallid grey houses.

Finally, after waiting and waiting crammed in like puppies in a basket, we moved off down the street. The houses became less dominating, set further apart, some without roofs, with tumble-down walls running between them, and then they stopped, and we were on the plain.

We followed a track for a few miles to a village called Colchani. From here I could see a distant shimmering strip just under the horizon ahead: the saltlake. The land was perfectly flat. The lorry stopped and people climbed out over the side to buy empanadas and limes and bread for the journey across the great saltlake, the Salar de Uyuni. When everyone was packed in tight again we pulled out of the village.

The ground on each side of the track was smooth, flat mud with white traces which gradually became stronger and more solid. Not far ahead the mud became an unbroken white. Then the saltlake itself came into view, its surface a pale blue mirror for as far as I could see. There was a film of brine over the salt and this reflected the sky immaculately. The track led into the water and disappeared like a slipway, once we had been launched.

The lorry churned through the few inches of salt water. We had escaped the clouds that brooded over Uyuni, at last, and I saw now that they were part of a tremendous ring of clouds that encircled the whole saltlake. Over to the right stood hundreds of little white pyramids. Each was reflected perfectly in the brine, so each was a diamond floating in the blue water. These were mounds of salt dug up to dry into hard cake.

All the Indians huddled beneath their blankets. The lorry was now a mass of striped colours broken only by a few woollen hats. They were like hibernating animals, shutting out the winter of the saltlake. I, at the back, caught the full force of the wind that tore over the lake, freezing even in the sunlight.

The saltlake was like a place half way between the earth and the sky. All around, in three dimensions, was blue. The air was thin and pure. The whole flat plain of brine seemed suspended above the earth. It was unlike anything I had ever seen or dreamt of, unearthly. The flat, flat blue, protected, hidden by the wide ring of clouds, was a great plateau strung up to the sky, held up to it, by its perfect reflection. It was a huge mirror. Across this infinite blue travelled the lorry, a nucleus of colours.

There was no visible horizon because the lake and the sky were the same colour. But all around, where there should have been a horizon, hovered diamond shapes, arrowheads, spearheads. These were the peaks of mountains with their reflections. The furthest away were deep blue and were distorted by the mirage which replaced the horizon; the nearer ones were mauve, then pink, then brown, the nearest green. All of these were suspended in the enormous sky.

Later we came on to dry salt. Now, looking around, it seemed that the whole saltlake was bone dry and white, as if the brine had been a mirage and vanished. The Salar was a great plate like the Flat Earth. From the abyss around the edge had grown up the huge mountains whose peaks peered over the rim. Islands grew out of the salt too, like smooth rocks on a dead calm sea, an unreal, frozen sea. The lorry hissed on the salt crust. On the vast sheet of white it was a tiny moving particle now, insignificant.

Then small patches of water appeared and the surface looked like a half-silvered mirror, with strips of normal glass between strips of mirrored glass. You could see the flitting patches of blue as constituting a continuous plain. The salt strips between them became thinner and thinner and finally gave way to a perfect mirror of water. Ahead a sharp mountain sat on its reflection. Further away, to the right of it, two dark blue hills hovered over their doubles. Imperceptibly we drew nearer to the tall mountain. Clouds hung above its peak and I could see it was a volcano.

It was like coming to an island in an ocean; a smooth green hill rising up at its top in the rocky walls of a crater. As we approached the shore I saw it was covered with green moss and a little way up the hill stood great crumbling chunks of rock tossed down by the volcano centuries ago. Stone walls laced the side of the hill for no apparent purpose, unless to enmesh the volcano.

The Indians came out from under their blankets as the lorry drove off the salt to stop on the rock-strewn mud of the shore.

There was a cluster of stone dwellings with thatched roofs at the foot of the volcano. People appeared among the houses. Scruffy children came running out with Victorian sticks and hoops which they chased down to the lorry. Some passengers climbed out. One was a woman with a wide-eyed child strapped to her back in a blanket; the child stared at me, bewildered by the life outside its earthen home.

I asked a man where we were.

'Tunupa,' he replied. The volcano was called Tunupa and the village was called Tunupa.

Now some men and women had walked nearer the lorry. They were silent and slow, isolated people bound to the hill on which their llamas grazed and their potatoes grew. For all the Aymaras the strongest bond is to the place where they live, the place that yields their sustenance. Their spirits are nearly all spirits of place, which inhabit their local fields and hills, and mountains are living bodies for them. So these villagers would worship Tunupa, the hill that fed them.

In fact, Tunupa is the name of the Aymara god of thunder. He is often believed to inhabit volcanoes. But it is also the

name of a character in Aymara myths who wandered the
length of the Andes telling people to love one another, not to
fight, to do good works, not bad. He urged the Indians to
abstain from chicha, their maize beer, and to take no more
than one wife. He travelled with five disciples. All six men
wore long robes and bushy beards and had blue eyes. They
were white men. Tunupa baptized Indians who were won
over to his moral code by sprinkling water on the forehead.
His mistake was to baptize the daughter of King Makuri. The
king was so angered by this that he drove Tunupa away,
having killed his disciples. Some say Tunupa was driven down
to the Pacific Ocean where he walked out on to the waves and
became 'Foam of the Sea', or *Viracocha,* creator-god of the
Aymaras. Others claim that he was put in a totora reed boat
and cast off into Lake Titicaca. His boat sailed so fast that
when it reached the other side of the lake it smashed through
the shore and thus formed the only river which flows down to
the Pacific from the Altiplano. Tunupa surfed down to the
ocean on the new stream.

Tunupa was a character of great interest to the early missionaries. The stories about him were proof that some of the
Apostles had reached the New World. Whether he himself
was Saint Thomas or Saint James was disputed, but it was
clear that the word of Christ had been heard in the Andes and
had been ignored, which did nothing to endear the Indians to
the Spaniards. Tunupa, then, had the last jab at the people
who had driven him out.

After a while the lorry ground on, away from Tunupa. It
followed a rugged track along the shore, making far slower
progress than it had done on the saltlake. We were under
clouds again, and Tunupa became a bleak and lonely Hebrid-
ean island. We rolled by another hamlet with a white church,
a feeble comfort against the quiet, brooding hills behind it and
the vast saltlake in front. This too might have been a Scottish
landscape, with its moors and grey sky.

Then, under the icy clouds, we rolled back on to the salt.
A cold wind was blowing fiercely. It was like one of the jet-

streams that race through the earth's upper atmosphere. The Indians hid their heads under the blankets and hoped to sleep. The sun and the sky were hidden by the clouds and the hills on the shore of the saltlake, over to our right, were green and desolate. By now it was late in the day. The lorry churned and hissed on. I saw that we were heading for an inlet between the hills of the western shore. The sun found a gap in the clouds and laid a gold carpet over the salt. The big hills on each side of the inlet were dark and glowed in the late rays. It was like the most beautiful Mediterranean bay, but somehow a little unearthly: as if this sea and the dark hills were too beautiful, too quiet, and the air between them too hazy and golden to be real. It might have been some visionary artist's impression of an Aegean dusk, an image charged with significance; it was better than the real thing.

The lorry left the salt, climbed up a rocky hill and over the crest and down, into Llica. The sun had disappeared behind a ridge ahead and it was getting dark. We entered the narrow streets between the small adobe houses with their thatched roofs and a group of children came scampering along in the wake of the lorry, the bravest boys holding on to the back, even hanging there, swinging along with their feet drawn up. When we reached the town plaza, a dusty slope among the houses in the centre of which stood an iron bandstand surrounded by a few scraggy plants, a crowd gathered round the lorry. They were quiet and reverent in the darkness, men and women standing about to wait for their relatives to climb out with all their bundles or simply to watch the arrival of the fortnightly mission from outside.

The first thing I had to do was report to the police station. It was a low concrete building at the top of the square. None of its lights worked. I found the three policemen standing in a black corridor. They were surprised to see a visitor.

'What is your intention in Llica?' enquired the Chief of Police.

'To see it,' I explained.

He was even more surprised; suspicious too. 'How long do you intend to stay?'

'Two or three days.'

He turned to his men. They were both smiling, their teeth white in the dark. 'How are you leaving?' he asked.

'In a lorry,' I said.

'On Monday or Tuesday? There's no lorry at least until next Saturday. It could be that there's one on Saturday going to Salinas.' Today was Sunday. What would I do for a week in this tiny town? He added: 'But there may not be one.'

One of the policemen took me across the square to the Lorry Drivers' Lodging House. This was where I was to stay. My room was a long corridor partitioned with walls of sack-cloth. It overlooked the plaza on one side, an ordinary family yard with chickens and a donkey on the other.

The next day I went to have breakfast in a small pension. The narrow dusty streets were almost deserted. I passed only two Chola women sitting on the doorsteps of shops. The sun was strong and the hills above the town glinted in the early light. The houses and their roofs were almost exactly the colour of the dirt streets, so that the whole town couldn't have been less conspicuous on the land. It was a quiet and sleepy place. There were too few inhabitants for the number of houses. Throughout the day it remained deserted. Some of the houses had no roofs; it was as if most of the population had abandoned the town.

A schoolteacher was the only other person who ate in the pension. He excused himself for not doing his own cooking and explained it was because he couldn't fit the time for it into his 'plan of work'. At lunch, when the woman that fed us waddled in with bowls of soup, he told me that the grain in the soup was *quinoa,* a high-altitude crop, and revealed his plan to persuade the whole Bolivian people to subsist on quinoa. It was pure protein, he said.

That evening I tried to buy a blanket. A man I had met in the plaza agreed to sell me one. So I went to his house where he spent half an hour pumping a kerosene lamp to get it as bright as he wanted. When he was finally satisfied he left it on the corner of a small billiard table—the only piece of furniture in the room—and fetched a typical blanket, black with bands of strong colour every few inches.

It was just what I wanted. We fixed a price and I was getting out the money when the man's wife stepped from a dark doorway into the circle of light sent out by the kerosene lamp. He and I were crouched next to the table with the blanket on the floor between us. She, with a sneering mouth and long plaits, came and stood silently behind him. Then she said something in Aymara.

He glanced up at her, smiled anxiously at me and said, 'I'm sorry. I can't sell it. *No puedo.*' He folded the blanket up.

'Why not?' I asked.

He shrugged his shoulders and repeated, 'No puedo.'

The woman reached down and took away the blanket.

'But I've got the money here,' I said. She disappeared into the darkness.

'I'm sorry,' said the man. There was evidently nothing he could do against his wife's will. She had the last say.

When I turned off my torch that night in my bedroom I looked out of the window on to the plaza. The town was as deserted as ever. In the blue moonlight, the bell-tower next to the church looked more like some elongated pre-Columbian pyramid than a piece of Christian architecture. The sky was clear, and the moon made the stars scarce. Beneath them the town seemed like a Near Eastern city; it even made me think of Bethlehem and the Nativity, with the crude adobe houses and the shining straw roofs. It was completely quiet. I climbed into bed, under several rough blankets which smelt of mules. I could still see the icy blue air outside and I felt cold.

Suddenly, in the middle of the night, I was woken by a little rap on the window and then a voice from the plaza below. I shivered under the blankets. The voice kept talking. A pebble came up and bounced off the windowpane again. So I got up and looked down.

A man in a suit and poncho was there. He waved up at me and called out: 'Vamos! Vamos!' Let's go!

'Where?' I asked.

'To Salinas. El azufrero is going to Salinas de García Mendoza.'

I had heard about the sulphur lorry from the policemen. It was the only lorry that might be going on from Llica within the fortnight. 'When?' I asked.

'Ahora! Ahora!' Now. 'Ahorita!' Which is the diminutive of now and lacks stark simplicity. It is vaguer, far more friendly to a Bolivian tongue.

I got up and packed and left. The moon had set. Without a word the man led me through the darkness to the lorry, up a side street. The engine was already running. There was space for me in the cabin along with the driver's wife and baby daughter.

'To Salinas, then,' confirmed the driver. Salinas was the next town to the east, inland from the shore of the Salar de Uyuni.

In the predawn light the saltlake was a mauve plate. When the sun rose we had moved on to brine, and a second sun sank beneath inverted mountains. The cab of the lorry was flooded with blinding light.

Finally we left the salt for the last time, to wind inland among hills for an hour. The driver pulled up where a track led off to the left. About a mile away a smoky cluster of eucalyptus trees shivered between the hills.

'Aya Salinas,' he said. This is how Bolivians pronounce allí, which means 'there'.

I climbed out. Already the sun had turned the night's frost to dust.

3

SALINAS DE GARCIA MENDOZA

BEFORE the reforms made by the National Revolutionary Movement in 1952 there used to be two kinds of inhabitants in Altiplano towns: *vecinos,* or neighbours, and *campesinos,* country folk. These terms are euphemisms. A *campesino* is an Indian. Even for an Indian the word 'Indian' is abusive. When his llama is stubborn he calls it Indio. The Indians lived in the communities clustered around town plazas.

'Neighbours' is a polite way of referring to the local gentry. They lived on the plazas. *Vecinos* were either mestizos, people of mixed blood, or they were Cholos. For the Cholos are hard to distinguish from the mestizos: after years under the Altiplano sun their complexions are the same and they wear the same clothes. A Cholo is an Indian who wears mestizo clothes; and mestizos wear suits like the whites. Social climbing is all a matter of dress. Put on a suit and you cease to be a *campesino*.

Only *vecinos* could attend meetings in the town hall. They controlled all town affairs. Among their number were the judge, the mayor and the priest.

After the revolution of 1952 a new system of local authority was set up. The new government sent agents with arms and ideology about the Altiplano to help overthrow the *vecinos* and establish the new *sindicatos*. These syndicates consisted of thirteen secretaries. Each secretary was in charge of a different aspect of community life. As the syndicates were meant to submit reports to the government they needed literate secretaries. They suffered consequently from a shortage of secretaries, the Altiplano having a very low literacy rate. This undermined their authority in the community, especially since all this time a far more important and far older hierarchy continued to flourish.

The *cargo* system is an ancient Andean institution. A *cargo* is a sponsorship of a fiesta. Fiestas aren't paid for by everyone. The beer, the food, the brass bands, the pipe bands, the spirits, the decorations, these are all free for the participants, for the whole community. Having to fish out money, to watch your purse, check your extravagance, would ruin a fiesta. But clearly someone has to foot the bill.

Every fiesta needs a patron. It's an honour to sponsor a fiesta, to bear its *cargo*. So great is the prestige that it's impossible to rise in the community without sponsoring fiestas. Some fiestas are more important than others, of course. Before a man can sponsor the fiesta of San Salvador he must have sponsored many lesser ones, and have been deemed to have done it well, with plenty of food and drink and good music. But how does he pay for all this? Surely if the people pooled their resources they could afford better fiestas?

There are two ways a man pays for this *cargo*. He saves. (White Bolivians say that the Indians of the Altiplano eat nothing but potatoes yet have thousands of dollars buried in their floors; they piss all the money away on wild drinking bouts.) And he gets help from his friends. They lend him money on the understanding that when they have a *cargo* he'll return the favour. This bond of mutual assistance is known as an *aini* bond. A man may spend lots of money on other people's fiestas before he even sponsors one himself: the more *aini* bonds he can develop by helping others out, the more money he'll be able to raise when his fiesta comes around.

The principle of the *cargo* is that the more you do for the community, the more it'll do for you. Give it a good fiesta and you rise in the hierarchy. Ultimately, if you ever manage to sponsor the biggest fiesta then you'll be in with a chance of becoming *jilakata* of the village, the traditional headman. The amount of honour that is bestowed on this man—he can settle disputes, people are ready to listen to him, even to agree with him (he can't actually command anyone to do anything)—requires a great deal of compensation. He has to forgo all other activities during the year that he is in office, so much of his time will be spent playing the host. He has to spend so much money too in this one year that he may use up all the *aini* debts he has accrued over the years. This is the problem of leadership among all the American Indians: so much is demanded of you that if you're rich enough to afford it you're sure to be the poorest man in the community after- wards. But by then you're a *pasado,* one who has passed, and allowed to rest on your laurels till you die.

The most lavish and magnificent fiestas ever seen in the Andes, of course, were those of the Inca emperor. When he wasn't extravagant enough, rebellion followed.

A stony track led up to Salinas de García Mendoza, past der- elict houses and long adobe walls. The morning shadows among the hills had evaporated, leaving behind rippled slopes of green that glistened like the flanks of a well-run horse. By the time I reached the main plaza I was hot and ready for the swimming shadows of its eucalyptus leaves.

I sat on a bench. The town seemed deserted. Two sides of

the square were occupied by very formal and ornate colonial buildings, a Palace of Justice and a *Policía:* Salinas had been a canton capital. Now it was top-heavy. The bulk of the town was in this square; outside there were just a few streets of adobe homes.

A man in a dusty suit and bowler appeared on the far side of the square. He stared at me for a minute, his head held back for scrutiny, then shuffled away down one of the side streets.

The police no longer used the grand white building; its ill-fitting doors were padlocked. But a Bolivian *Policía* escutcheon hung above a doorway on the other side of the plaza. Under it a short dark corridor gave into a courtyard full of rows of adobe bricks stacked so they leaned against one another like dominoes. There were some wooden moulds lying on the ground too: this was an adobe factory.

'Buenos días,' I called out, not wanting to be caught trespassing on police property. A distant cock crowed. But I did need to find someone. I had to find where to stay, where to eat, and to get rid of my things. So I climbed a staircase attached to the wall and stepped into a long room overlooking the plaza. It was some kind of boardroom, dark and empty with a varnished floor. Chairs stood around the walls, a desk at one end. Behind the desk was a glass door.

Suddenly the door opened. The top half of an old man with white hair appeared. 'Buenos días,' he exclaimed. He was grinning delightedly. 'Pase, pase,' he beckoned me vigorously, 'pase, no más.' Do no more than come in.

It was a tiny room. There were seven other men inside, all in tatty suits impregnated with dust—it's the wind on the Altiplano that sends the dust into everything—and all in their late middle age. Their sun-tightened faces creased into smiles as each was introduced. I had stumbled upon splendid company: there was the Corregidor or chief magistrate, the mayor, a Secretary General, a Secretary of Public Works, a Secretary of Football, and three other important secretaries.

Some stood, some sat. There wasn't much space in that

little room. I had to remove my rucksack before entering. Why didn't they use the empty committee room? Because the typewriter was kept in here. In front of it sat the Secretary of Relations.

The town officials were pleased and excited by my arrival. As politely as he could one asked to see my passport and handed it to the Secretary of Relations who studied it intently before snapping down his bail bar on a sheet of lined paper. They all smiled, in case I should be offended by the formalities.

Was there an *alojamiento*, I asked, a hotel?

'No hay alojamiento, pues,' said one who was holding his hat meekly in front. 'Pues' means nothing more than 'then'; but everyone says it in Bolivia. And often they abbreviate it to a little noise added to the end of words: 'ps'. So instead of Sí, you sometimes hear Síps.

'But we will prepare a bed for you.' Everyone nodded and smiled in reverent silence as the typing was done.

'You can eat at the Corregidor's house. His wife will give you food,' said one. 'Come back a little later and we'll show you your room.'

'Muchas gracias, señores.' All their tight faces nodded appreciatively.

I went back out into the square. I lumbered over to a shop. A woman was sitting in the doorway, her skirts spread wide over the step. I walked past her. The shop was dark after the bright sun outside. She got up slowly and waddled over to the wooden counter.

'Qué cosita quiere?' she asked. What little thing would I like? Her mouth was set in a nasty sneer.

'Do you have any oranges?'

'No hay.'

On the counter there were some fruits which looked very like oranges, on a piece of cloth.

'What are those?' I asked.

'Limas,' she said, not looking at me, her top lip drawn up as if she had bitten something disgusting.

49

'Cuánto cuesta?' I asked.

'Five for each one.' It was far too high.

'Is it possible for less?' I tried.

'No,' she said shortly and quietly, looking to her side.

I bought some Chiclet bubble-gum instead and walked out into the square. A man waved from the other side, beckoning. He was one of the officials, the tallest one, who could almost have passed for a gangster in his well-fitting suit if it hadn't been filthy. He had a long kind face. He was called Don Panamá Saturnino. He told me to follow him, leading me down a street to a small newly-built adobe house with a corrugated iron roof. He unlocked the door. It was bare inside, with two beds and a table.

'This is for you.'

'Muchas gracias, señor.'

'This is my house. I live up near the square but this is my house too.' He waved his arms as he spoke.

'How much shall I pay?'

He burst out: 'Nothing. No, no, nada, nada.' Then: 'But you have a camera?'

'Yes.'

'Can you take a photograph?'

'Yes.'

He opened the back door and beckoned me outside. There was an unobstructed view of a large rounded hill baking under a dark blue noon sky.

'It's my mountain. Can you take a photograph of it?'

'Of course,' I said.

'Bueno, bueno,' he was delighted. 'It has gold,' he nodded slowly, mysteriously. 'One day I'm going to make a mine here. Then I'll go to London. Why don't you bring money and equipment from your country? We can make a mine together. The mountain is *full* of gold.'

The following day the Corregidor's son took me up a volcano a little way from the town. He was light and nimble, a lad of fourteen, his black hair flopping about his skull as he scampered between the rocks. He had to stop and wait for me every twenty yards. In my stout boots every step was an exertion and I still wasn't used to the altitude. Inhabitants of the Altiplano have bigger lungs than the rest of humanity. I ate the bread and limes he had brought along before we were half way up. Gradually the mud flats at the edge of the Salar de Uyuni came into view far away beyond the litter of houses below, and then a winking strip of sky showed beneath the far mountains: the saltlake itself.

We moved out on to a wide sloping curve, an enormous camber. It was studded with short spreading kechuara trees, like dwarf mesquites. No higher than a man, they have thin black trunks which writhe up to a spread of branches putting forth dry leaves. They're the shape of umbrellas.

The Corregidor's son went about gathering tussocks of straw which he bunched round the base of a kechuara. When there was a thick collar around the scraggy neck of the trunk he set fire to it. In a moment there was a single broad flame of orange which roared fiercely. In the sunlight it was a translucent flame, very hot. But no sooner was the whole bush burning in the single ghostly flame than the thundering hiss began to fade, the leap of the flame to slacken. The fuel was dry but meagre. Already the fire died, leaving a silver and black corpse.

'Why?' I asked.

'To scare off the pumas and condors,' said the boy. He swung his bag over his shoulder again. His movements were all limp but definite, just as his body was thin but agile. He always looked as if he might topple or be blown over. In fact he was surefooted as a goat.

The crater we were making for was always just over the next brow. He kept telling me of two German scientists who had visited the crater some time in the past. I never saw anything ahead that could have been the outer walls of a volcanic cauldron, and in the end I never saw the crater. The Corregidor's son stopped and raised his eyes attentively as if trying to hear a distant voice.

'It's late,' he said. 'We have to return. It's four o'clock.' He had no watch and he hadn't even looked at the sun. He had plucked the time out of the air, and got it right.

We descended a different way. The clay-red potato fields behind Salinas appeared below, stretching from the scattered houses up the valley until it became narrow and turned a bend. Then we came upon a cluster of *chullpas* strung along a rock-strewn ridge.

Chullpas are thought to be burial chambers. They are circular houses built of stone long before the Incas. Some are as tall as thirty feet, huge cylinders on the plain. These ones were a yard high and a yard wide, little stone tubs. Each had a hole at ground level, a diminutive doorway.

'That,' said the Corregidor's son, 'is the entrance. The *Chullpares*'—the Chullpa People—'weren't even a metre high. They were tiny people. Pequeñitos,' he stressed.

I was impressed, not as yet by the myth of this ancient race, but by what seemed an inexplicable urge—to build houses for the dead high on a bleak ridge. This was a little necropolis up here, a village for the dead way above the living town. People get homes of dried mud, but the dead get dwellings of immortal stone up near the sky.

I tried to ask more about these Chullpare people, but the boy grew nervous. His black eyes darted about suspiciously. He didn't want to linger on the subject. He had said his say: they were very small people from long ago.

Lower down the boy pulled a small revolver from his trouser pocket. It was a light gun with a slender handle, a simple gun. He also had a handful of cartridges. He told me to be still. He had seen a viscacha.

He moved forward crouching, and then stopped. There on a rock below I saw it, a little mammal like a rabbit and like a chipmunk, golden-coloured and palpitatingly alert. As the lad levelled his barrel the thing darted out of sight into its world of passages beneath the rocks. The boy moved forward further and waited patiently. Like a dolphin the animal would resurface to the world of light before long. Sure enough it did, but too far away for a shot.

That evening at supper in the dark room lit by one candle in the Corregidor's house I tried to talk to him about the chullpas. He was hardly more informative than his son. His soft black eyes in the candle flame grew harder, anxious, and he shyly told me that when the Chullpares lived there was no sun. At that time there had been only the moon. A diviner told the Chullpares of the coming sun. So they built the chullpas with the doors facing east, ready for the dawn. But when it came they all died. I asked what he meant and he was beginning to explain to me about four ages of the world, one of which, preceding this one, had been the Age of the Moon, when his wife called him from just outside the door. He was glad of the excuse and said, 'Permiso,' apologetically as he rose.

He came back in with his wife immediately behind. She was a witch-like woman with long black plaits made longer by tassels of oily wool woven into the strands at the ends. She wasn't wearing her hat. She had a severe parting. She leaned forwards on the end of the table. Her face was pallid in the candlelight.

'How can you help us?' she asked, quietly and icily.

I said I didn't understand her question and the Corregidor, very embarrassed, rephrased it for me.

'I'll send many things from England,' I lied.

'Can you make us a loan?' The corners of her mouth were drawn up in that characteristic sneer of the women.

I was taken aback. I said I didn't understand.

'Ah,' she stared at me long and hatefully, or so it seemed.

I ate up and said goodnight. As I walked back to my room from the Corregidor's house just off the plaza I looked up at the moon. It was bright and nearly full. Suddenly the whole town became strange and sinister. The adobe houses were small hollow heads; their straw roofs were crude wigs. The church was a primitive phosphorescent monster. The women of this town were witches, guardians of an arcane religion, a cruel moon-worship. In their absurd, wide, ballerina-like skirts and derby hats, with their wrinkled, worn faces, the women held a frightening dominion over the men. And they didn't want me here. They didn't want me prying into their beliefs.

The moon filled the empty streets with cold light. Tomorrow it would be full. All about the town the silvery hills basked in their former glory. The little Chullpares were leaping among them. What was I doing in such a remote place? Worst of all, there was to be a religious ceremony next day.

It was a relief to see the sun in the morning. But during the night someone had laid out straw all along the top of the wall enclosing my house's compound and on the wall facing my front door. Or had they done it in the first hour of the morning, silently? Or had I failed to notice it last night? And why had they carefully balanced straw on these walls? Why? Was it something to do with the ceremony that would be held tonight, at the full moon?

On the way to breakfast women sitting on their doorsteps grudgingly muttered 'Buen día' as I passed. It was Good Friday. The Corregidor's daughter, an energetic girl of thirteen, brought in my mug of coffee and little flat loaf of bread. As ever, she had the baby curled in her arm. Wherever she looked a second pair of eyes looked too; whenever her smooth supple face was seen a second face, with huge amazed eyes and a crust of dried phlegm under its nose, was seen too. She was training to be a mother. And the baby was being weaned of its mother's company. (Babies are weaned of the teat abruptly, at the age of two. On the day that infancy is to end mothers smear their nipples with rancid guinea-pig fat.)

'What's happening tonight?' I asked her. She'll be honest, I thought.

'The Procession,' she said with an inane grin.

'What's that?'

'It's the Procession.'

'What time does it begin?'

'Begins at eight.'

Later in the morning I saw a hot and dusty woman seated against a wall with her knees drawn up into the slither of shade. She was in the position that Andean corpses used to be buried in, and in which the mummies still sit, chin on the knees. She was wearing a black dress with heavy golden embroidery around its hem. A black shawl was held in place by her derby. She was a Quechua. She had come in from a community in the hills behind Salinas. Her hands were fantastically wrinkled, hardly like the human hands that I knew. She couldn't take her eyes off me as I walked by. It didn't matter if I stared back. She was immune in her own astonishment and exhaustion.

During the afternoon activities stepped up in the town. Several altars were erected in the plaza and nearby streets. There were tables with backboards draped in blankets and covered with decorations: gilt-framed pictures of the Virgin, eucalyptus sprigs, balls of silver foil, cutlery, plates, anything colourful. One was covered with a white sheet festooned with leaves and twigs. Pictures of the two local saints were hanging on it. A small group was standing around the altar, adding items to it and rearranging them and staring on idly. I watched too, and said to them all how beautiful it looked. They went about their business more sullenly, eyes downcast. They didn't want me around.

At about six o'clock I went to have supper. To the west, between the adobe houses, you could see the golden dusk in the air and darkness drawing in. But to the east, the moon was already up, full and swollen, and the roofs of the houses were beginning to show a faint sheen. I saw that it would never get dark tonight, that dusk would hand the streets over to moonlight directly, without a mediating darkness. Now, in this eerie mixture of the two poles of light, the houses metamorphosed into different creations: they became stark staring faces, like fearful primitive carvings.

In the Corregidor's house the big table on which I ate had been taken away. A collapsible one was in its place. The Corregidor had given it up for an altar he was sponsoring this evening. Two tin plates of rice and stew were brought in the darkness and when the Corregidor himself came in a few minutes later with a candle under his face I was surprised to see my food was yellow and not brown. The Corregidor was smiling, his eyes thin with drooping lids. He put the candle on the table.

'Buenas noches,' he said. 'Qué tal?' How are you?

'Bueno, bueno,' I replied.

'What did you think of the supper?'

'Rico, rico,' I said. Delicious.

'Rico, no?' he asked. He was anxious to keep the conversation to this topic, I thought.

'Sí, muy rico.' Very delicious.

'Buen entonces—' he said. Well then . . . He was standing with his hands held together in front. He doesn't want to mention the Procession, I was thinking. I'll have to.

'Señor, what time does the Procession begin?'

'Well, seven or eight or thereabouts, it should be. But it's nothing. Nothing much will happen.'

All I wanted now was a reassurance that it wouldn't be an infringement of the town's privacy, or dangerous, for me to watch the Procession. But none came. Instead the ceremony seemed a guarded secret; anything could happen.

I lingered along with a few others in the plaza. Through the open door of the church I could see the yellow light inside and the crowd beneath it. There was a stir near the altar, at the far end, and then I could make out a statue bobbing up and down above the heads of the crowd. The painfully thin and high voices of singing Indian women grew louder and the statue, a local saint dressed in deep blue with shining porcelain cheeks, came out of the door into the churchyard, out of the light into the cold night. The singing women followed it, along with a man carrying a lantern to light their way. They were contracting their throats and forcing the notes out in a cat-like squeal; they considered this the correct and reverent way to sing. They passed through the gates of the yard and started round the plaza.

It was an enormous relief to see that the Procession was Catholic. But then among the last people following the saint, before they had reached the gates, there appeared a troupe of white figures. Out into the street they bore a glass chest containing a pale effigy of Christ taken down from the cross and wrapped in white rags like swaddling clothes. They were wearing white masks that looked as though they were real faces which had been smeared with white clay. White smocks hung down to their knees. Then the boom of a drum broke across the thin wailing of the women, immediately followed by the piercing jangle of several trumpets missing their notes but blasting away nevertheless, and of euphoniums blown so hard that even they were made to rasp like pained beasts. Nevertheless the tune they played, in a minor key, was sad and noble, a funeral march. It filled the town and was sent up into the night to sail over to the chullpas and the hills around. It completely drowned the women, and it wasn't until a third effigy had passed right beside me that I realized there was another chorus of women too, behind this figure, the other local saint clad in scarlet.

The thick line of people slowly moved round the plaza, each procession stopping in its turn at three of the corners where altars had been set up, pockets of light in the dark square. Clouds of incense billowed up from each, and the band would stop for a while as Latin prayers were murmured by a priest at the head of its procession so that the feeble singing of the women could be heard again coming from two sides of the square, like the whinings of two clouds of mosquitos.

I went ahead to an altar which the leading group was about to leave. Back down the street at the next corner smoke was drifting up in clouds, fitfully illuminated by the few stars of light around the altar, the kerosene lamps, and then disappearing in the dark above the houses. The band rang out in the night, drowning out the hymn of the women beside me as they began to move on again. I saw a white figure in breeches and short smock lurching towards me. He was leading the band's procession, lumbered with the awkward weight of an immense cross. Lit up from behind by the lights at the head of the group he looked like some ghostly jester forced to walk in front of a jeering crowd. It was Christ bearing his cross; and then a little later the deathly figures carrying his dead body in the glass chest. It was his funeral procession.

Or was he a *yatiri,* this man in white? The yatiris, the white witches of the Altiplano, wear white robes and their novices white smocks. And the processions of people—were these like the pagan funeral rites of the Altiplano, when all the members of a community fall in behind the corpse of the deceased on its passage to the grave, singing on the way? And the little things wrapped in silver foil on the altars—offerings to Ekkekko, the god of the household. The Virgin and Saints weren't the only objects of worship.

Suddenly, as I was gazing at the deathly Christ-figures, a party of boys ran up to me. Their black mops of hair shone like tar and their eyes sparkled. They took my hands, seven or eight of them reaching in on both sides to touch me. I had been trying to watch the proceedings as discreetly as possible, pressed against a door in a wall. The boys pulled me out into the middle of the street, right in front of the lumbering Christ, the leader of the main procession. My arms were spread out from my body, their little hands repeatedly clutching and slipping on my fingers as they jostled one another for access to the skin of the stranger. Like a mothering sow I hurried to the open plaza.

Clutches of dark figures along the edge of the street and under the trees of the plaza watched me. But no one seemed to mind. The boys dispersed without so much as mentioning Chiclet, their usual plea.

Later on when the crowd had snaked its way back into the church, its atmosphere so dense with the smell of incense that it filled your head as you breathed, the women sang a hymn and the rest fidgeted and chatted in the unlit pews. The band, lounging at the back of the church, blew the odd note to see if they could pick up the tune. The Corregidor invited me up to the front to sit with all the officials beneath the blue robes of one of the saints reinstated on his pedestal after his round of the town. The secretaries all leaned forward to nod at me and smile, and gave me cigarettes and coca leaves and asked what I thought of the Procession. All the while the insipid, high voices of the women went round the church. Huddled in the pews, they were a mass of clothes in the darkness. Their eyes shone. They would stop for a while, and speech would echo round the church like whispers, and then start again on some long and repetitive hymn. This half-hearted ceremony was to continue all night. The Indians of the Altiplano always hold wakes for the dead.

I left Salinas in the morning. As I was walking out of the town a white Bolivian in modern dress came the other way. He hailed me, shook my hand, asked what I was doing here. He had just arrived in Salinas to do some agricultural research. He was called Oscar. He came from the Instituto Boliviano de Transformacion Agricultural in Oruro, and knew the Altiplano well. He had a tanned face, broad but with a pointed nose and small, prominent cheekbones. He smiled little; he was deeply concerned about the Indians of the Altiplano. Their diet was very poor.

I asked him about the people of the communities in the hills, like the woman I had seen the previous morning in her native dress.

'If you want to see interesting indigenous people,' he said, 'people still leading very ancient lives that date from long before the Incas, go to the Departamento of Potosí. Here, I'll give you the name of my colleague in Oruro. He's going out there soon. You can ask him to take you.' This was a very fortunate meeting.

It was Saturday, and the lorry the policeman in Llica had mentioned would be passing Salinas on its way to Challapata. Challapata is on the main road north-south that crosses the Altiplano. This road is a mere dirt track used by lorries to ferry Indians from town to town: the railway line provides almost as much transport as the region requires. But the road is still a link to cities and therefore to civilization. Now that I was returning to it, Challapata had assumed the status of a port: it was a haven, a refuge of safety from the wide open spaces, and from the strange people among whom I was moving. And once I reached Challapata I would be able to reach a city.

Three women had already walked out from Salinas down the long track by which I had first entered the town. They sat beside bundled-up blankets at the junction with the track from Llica, three heaps of dusty clothes under the bleaching sun. I came and stood nearby, leaning against the roughness of an adobe wall, behind the women's backs. The nearest one rested her left elbow on her left knee and gazed to the right, up the track. Her mouth opened and closed as she rearranged coca leaves with her tongue. It made a clicking noise. I thought she would turn more to look at me. She didn't: though I had arrived from behind the women already knew who I was.

I waited in the sun. It would be no use asking the women when the lorry would come. If they replied at all they would say: 'Ahorita'; right now, like Don Panamá Saturnino had when he warned me of the coming truck.

An hour passed. Then suddenly I heard an engine and at once a shining, grinning, scarlet lorry appeared round a bend.

The driver wanted breakfast in Salinas. 'Ya no hay,' the women whined to him: the pension had closed down. So we all climbed into the back of the lorry, the old wooden sides leaning heavily as we did so. Ten women sat in the back, and no men. They were all going to the market at Challapata.

That day we had three punctures. Each time, the driver jumped out with a shovel and dug himself a little mound of earth just behind the lorry. With his friend shouting directions he would attempt to reverse one back wheel up on to the mound. Then the friend and he would realize that it would be easier if the lorry were lighter, so they would tell all the passengers to get out. Being plump and stiff, the women are never quick at climbing over the sides of lorries. If the back of a lorry can be opened they will always wait and use that. But this one didn't. The bolt had got bent and jammed. The sides were the only escape. As a woman reached the ground she would let go of the wooden wall; which would allow it to heave over the opposite way. And as the left and right walls were linked to one another by the front and back walls this would make the opposite wall fall out suddenly beneath the fingers and knees of whoever was climbing over it. The women soon learned that they must leave the truck one at a time. It would be half an hour before it was empty of its human contents. Then the driver would roll back and forth on and off his little mound till he had got the wheel exactly where his friend wanted it. It was a double wheel: they had to position the lorry so the inner tyre rested on the mound while the outer tyre was just free of it: this was the one that kept puncturing. They would take it off, bounce on the ends of spanners and screwdrivers, hands on each other's shoulders, to lever out the tyre rims, then pull out the inner tube and roll it in the dust, pump it with a bicycle pump, lick it in places, spit on it, fold it up, listen, spit more, listen again. Then the driver would pull a bicycle puncture repair kit from his trouser pocket.

His glue took an hour or more to dry. The women would sit on the ground munching corn. Then all would be reassembled. The lorry would be rolled off the mound; the women would reinstate themselves among their bundles of merchandise, one at a time. And we could proceed.

But the track was rutted and potholed. One after another the wheels dropped into holes. It was as if the lorry were a four-footed creature, walking slowly, heavily. With every step its wooden walls fell creaking out to one side. Always it seemed that the next time they would have to break off under their own weight.

Night fell as we were waiting for the glue to dry for the third time. Two of the women were grand enough to be chatting in Spanish. They agreed that we were about half way to Challapata. This meant we had made fifty miles in the day.

The world meanwhile cast a dark blue strip of shadow above the eastern horizon. Into this band rose a huge, blurred moon, quivering and elliptical and crimson. It was like an old shaggy rose. By the time all the women were back in the lorry the moon had risen into a brilliant porcelain coin. The Altiplano became silk reaching away to small dark folds in the distance. We dozen people had the plain to ourselves.

We couldn't drive right through the night because of the curfew, not that the driver would have wanted to anyway. We stopped before midnight to sleep in the truck, at the edge of a small village. We were moving again by dawn. And we reached Challapata by mid-morning.

Almost at once I was in another lorry heading north up the main road. For my destination was Oruro, the city which is the hub of the southern Altiplano, and in the course of the journey I had developed a real craving for a city, for civilization, for steaks and spirits and telephones and bedclothes, for cars, buses, pastries, fruits, newspapers. So I had no time for a small market town like Challapata. And besides, Oruro was only a couple of hours away.

4

CHIPAYAS

ORURO is built at the bottom of a hill. As you approach from the south the city glints in the sunlight like rubbish tossed down the hillside. Then suddenly you see a vendor standing at the side of the road, and another, and now there are side streets running off the road and at every corner a boy or a young woman with a tray of cigarettes and sweets. The intermittent houses congeal. Market stalls spring up along the street and thicken as you near the centre until all the streets are lined with stall after stall and behind every stall sits a Chola woman. The city is given up to marketing.

When you walk around Oruro, the streets filled with dust and sunlight and people, shouts come from the stalls all around: 'Qué cosita quiere? Qué quiere?' Everyone is there either to buy or to sell. As you pass the fruit stalls, line upon line of them out in the road, huge piles of oranges and limes and avocado pears stacked on the ground, the women shout, 'Qué cosita quiere? Naranja? Hay. Lima? Hay. Palto? *Hay!*' The last word, so seldom heard without its customary adjunct 'No', rings out with great delight, singing the difference between this bustling city and the little towns of the remoter south. Here the market women have everything in abundance: no slow waiting for goods to arrive or for crops to ripen. Here in Oruro everything is available and for sale. 'Qué quiere? Hay! Hay!'

Oruro is a city of dust and business and colour. The air is filled with shouts and car horns; the city buses, *micros*, painted any colour the driver fancies, push through the crowds blaring their horns continually; the railway line runs right through the centre of town, along the middle of a dusty street, flanked by fruit stalls which here are no more than baskets or sheets spread on the ground stacked with fruit and shaded by crude umbrellas of sticks and sackcloth. Everywhere there are Chola women, with their bowler hats and garish clothes. Occasionally, among the throng, a Cholo man moves under the weight of a great sack of potatoes; along the side of the street, between stalls, stand a few Cholo men, overawed.

Adobe houses straggle up the hill beside Oruro until it becomes too steep. They are exactly the same reddy brown as the earth: made of the earth and inconspicuous on it, like the houses of any remote settlement on the Altiplano. In most streets lorries stand waiting to take marketers back to their villages at the end of the day or next day. Oruro has grown up around its market; roads reach out from it on to the surrounding plain, drawing the goods. Houses sprawl along the roads for a while and then give up. All the magnetism is to the centre. The edges of the town, too far from it, are frayed.

As soon as I had found a hotel room in Oruro I went out to buy avocados. I ended up buying only one: it was the size of a watermelon. To go with it I bought a jar of Hellman's mayonnaise, the only American product I saw anywhere in the markets of Oruro. I ate the whole avocado for lunch, and was sick. It was months before I could face another one.

The hotel had a shower. The water pipe passed through a small electric heater. If too much water went through it too fast then it didn't get heated up. To have it hot the shower had to be a miserable trickle which would have made a man filling a small glass impatient. To have a decent stream of a shower you had to have it cold. But it was still a shower, and the first I had had in Bolivia.

In the evening I went to a bar that served *Yintonica*, or gin and tonic, and steak and chips. Why such perfectly English fare was to be found in Oruro I never knew. The owner was a white Bolivian from La Paz. Perhaps he had diplomatic friends in the capital, who had influenced his taste, though otherwise his bar-restaurant was chic in an American way: hamburgers and ice creams were its main attractions. It was by far the most cosmopolitan place in Oruro.

The next day I went along to the Bolivian Institute for Agricultural Transformation. The Institute was in a modern building just off the central plaza of Oruro, a quiet place with a few railed-in flowerbeds and bushes. Here I met Gonzalo Lazaro, who was the colleague of Oscar, the man I had met in Salinas.

Gonzalo was an agronomist from La Paz. He had spent three years out on the Altiplano, though his young-looking face didn't show it. He was a white Bolivian, with middle-brown hair, and wore tidy, modern western clothes. He had learned English at school and insisted on seeing how much he could remember. Generally it was very little, but it took him a long time to accept this. Sometimes his sentences took five or ten minutes to produce. Yet he refused to be prompted, and only after long effort would he revert to Spanish. I stood talking an hour or more in the concrete and tiled office of the Institute. The final message was that he would love to take me to the Departamento de Potosí to visit remote Indian communities, but his jeep had broken down. I would have to wait until the required part arrived from La Paz. This would probably be in a week's time. So why didn't I firstly come along to his house to read his books about Bolivian Indians, and then go on a four- or five-day trip to a fantastic village out on the western Altiplano, near Chile? When I returned we would go into Potosí.

'Which village is this?' I asked.

'Chipaya. The Chipayas are the last of the Urus, the oldest Indians of the Altiplano; maybe in all South America. They still have a Stone Age technology. But why not come back to my house at lunchtime? You can read about the Chipayas then.' He added in English: 'Bery, bery . . . er . . . aha . . . interst,' pronouncing the last word with great difficulty, as if it were all consonants.

The name 'Oruro' is an elision of 'Uru-Uru'. Both the city and a lake nearby earned this title because many Uru Indians used to live in the area; but on the bleak Altiplano it isn't a title of which to be proud, for the Urus are the most despised Indians of the central Andes. The Aymaras call them ugly, dirty, thick; 'kinchacatati', which means big-livered, and 'chancumankkeri', eaters of water-weeds. For the Urus used to inhabit the shores of the rivers and lakes of the Altiplano. Some even say they lived in holes underneath the reed-beds. Perhaps that was why they stank. And they speak an idiotic language, *poquina*, which no one else on the Altiplano can understand. (The language is of unique stock and was used as a code by the Americans in Vietnam.) And they are arrogant. They claim to be the oldest race on earth, older even than the sun. But the Aymaras know better: the Urus emerged from the slime of Lake Titicaca when the sun first rose.

No wonder they were an untouchable caste in the Aymara kingdoms. They had their use, of course. No one else liked routing among the reeds for birds' eggs and eels. But they were lower than the lowest Aymaras, a specialist breed allowed to live on as long as they functioned in their proper manner as fishermen. One Aymara king even sent a number of Urus down to make a colony on the Pacific coast. He liked dried ocean fish.

Are the Urus especially talented fishermen? No. They do have some ingenious labour-saving traps, but their chief qualification is willingness. For an Aymara, the land is not merely a source of sustenance, it's a living deity, Pacha Mama (or Earth Mother). To forsake agriculture is to turn one's back on Pacha Mama; almost to become a heathen. So Aymara fishermen are few, or ought to be. (In fact there are plenty of them. But even these lowest Aymaras look down on the Urus, their fellow labourers. They are blinded by prejudice.)

Today there are almost no Urus left. The lakes of the Altiplano became saltlakes and like newts the amphibious Urus died out. But there is one settlement by the swamps of Coipasa out in the west of the Altiplano, Chipaya, where an Uru subgroup still survives. After the 1952 revolution the new government heard about this last settlement of Urus, and learning that the Urus were allegedly the earliest Indians on the Altiplano resolved to help them: for they too were citizens in the new reformed nation of Bolivia. So a plaza was built on the incomparably bleak pampa near the Coipasa salt swamps. This plaza was a square of concrete bungalows with a flagpole in the middle.

The Chipayas have always lived in apparently random clusters of dwellings, many of which have been deserted over the centuries so that the whole plain around there is littered with homes and the shells of homes. Their houses are always cylinders of mud with conical roofs of mud or of straw, which collapse or rot if left untended: the abandoned dwellings are the roofless ones. In the midst of this wide field of mud structures the government built its plaza and called it Chipaya, and declared Chipaya a canton, a township.

The idea was to give the tribe a sense of identity which might preserve it in the face of modern influence and natural decay. The government were worried they might lose all their Urus altogether; so would the world. To encourage people to move to the plaza, food and seed-potatoes were distributed there by a government agents. A tractor was donated to the township. Agriculture would flourish.

The Chipayas left their homes. They built new ones all round the plaza. They ate the government food so they no longer bothered to hunt flamingoes in the swamps. Agents planted potatoes for them. They could ride on the tractor to the shops of Escara, the nearest village on the road to Oruro. Chipaya life undoubtedly improved, while the workload dwindled. Why work any more? Why hunt? Why plant? They don't need to any more. They were special, and the government told them so.

For the first time in their history the Urus were being favoured by outsiders and were not so stupid as to refuse the help. For the first time they embraced their role in an extraneous political regime. Even the Incas had left the Chipayas alone. They had had no need of an empty salty pampa too high to be cultivable. One Inca had once demanded a tribute from the Chipayas: they sent him lice.

A church has also been built in Chipaya. They don't mind at all. The church tower has become one of their three most powerful spirits.

It was a late afternoon when I set out in a lorry from Oruro for Escara, the nearest village to Chipaya that vehicles can reach. Just to the west of Oruro lies Lake Uru-Uru. It is now so shallow that large stretches of the surface are hard ground, and the track out to the west runs right through the middle of it. Under the late sun the lake was calm except here and there where long-beaked black birds made quiet ripples as they ducked for fish. Patches of moss and grass broke up the surface. The lake is a saltlake in the making, shallower than ever before.

Blue and orange clouds hung ahead over the horizon of the flat plate of the Altiplano. In our lorry there were only eight other passengers, all but one of them Chola women. Three had infants strapped on their backs in blankets. The other was a young man in a poncho who stood leaning against the back of the lorry beside me. He had very smooth, tight skin. Beneath his poncho he wore slacks and gym shoes: though he was an Indian he had spent time in Oruro, I guessed. I wasn't surprised when he started talking to me in Spanish.

'Where are you going?' he wanted to know.

'Chipaya.'

'Why?'

'I've heard it's interesting.'

'It is. I am a Chipaya. My parents moved from Chipaya to Escara twenty years ago, before I was born. But my blood is Chipaya.'

He was called Xavier. He was studying at the university in Oruro. As he spoke he would glance at me with uneasy, intelligent eyes.

'The Chipayas are the oldest people in the Andes, in all South America,' he said quietly, confidentially. 'There used to be Urus all over the Altiplano. Now only the Chipayas. You know why? There was a great famine. This is what the Chipayas say. A great famine killed all the Urus. You know why? Because the sun rose. When the Urus lived there was no sun. Then God transformed the world and started the Age of the Sun. The sun rose and made a famine and killed all the Urus. This is what the Chipayas say.'

This myth was just like the myth of the Chullpares back in Salinas de García Mendoza. Perhaps they too had been Urus.

Night was descending by the time we reached the Río Lauca, a wide brown river. Everyone climbed out and sat on the dry mud bank. A little convoy of vessels set out from far upstream of us on the opposite shore: one raft punted by men with immensely long poles, and two small rowing boats. The river was at least a hundred yards wide. As the craft laboured across, the current did its work too and brought them to land exactly at the mud ramp that had been smoothed into our bank. The driver greeted the raftsmen, shouting and laughing as they made fast on stakes driven into the ground. The men in the rowing-boats sat at their oars watching the lorry make its way on to the raft, and then out on to the water.

69

Once it was well out into the stream the rowers called us to their boats and we passengers followed the lorry over, the brown river lapped over our gunwales. The floating lorry turned on eddies and the punters ran around it to drop their poles at different sides. I could hear their cries and laughter.

Downstream stood the crumbled concrete pillars that had supported the bridge which used to span the river, till a rare spate pushed it over. And by the track as it continued on the other bank sprawled an encampment of sacking tents, where the raftsmen and oarsmen lived.

Xavier said: 'I'll tell you why the Chipayas weren't killed along with all the other Urus. When the sun rose one Uru couple decided to hide in the waters of the Río Lauca. The river protected them from the sun. So they only came out of the waters at night, under the moon. This is how they lived every day, hiding in the water, coming out at night. They were the only people to survive the sun's drought. They were the ancestors of the Chipayas. They were the first Chipayas.'

'And did the animals hide in the river, too, a pair of each?' I asked.

'Sí, sí, sí,' Xavier nodded vigorously.

Bolivian archaeologists support the Chipaya myths. They say that the reason the Chipayas have survived while the rest of the Urus have not is that the area they inhabit beside the Río Lauca has been slower to dry up than elsewhere. The whole western half of the Altiplano bears the scars of the climatic change it has undergone: the saltlakes, residues of inland seas, the wide, stony riverbeds which now hold only thin seasonal streams of brown water, the sprinkling of coarse shrubs and grasses the only vegetation the parched earth can support. The llamas have left this land and the flamingoes have flown away in search of new lakes. But the Chipayas' swamps beside the Salar de Coipasa have been kept watered by the Lauca. So their myths acknowledge their debt: the river has saved them.

I slept on the earth floor of Xavier's house in Escara. Xavier's uncle had an old bicycle which I could use to go to

Chipaya. It was a day to walk, but would only take a morning to get there on a bicycle. But first he had to bandage up the back tyre where it threatened to swell out of the rim. He wrapped an old inner tube round and round the tyre, between the spokes.

The track was soft sand between the shrubs. It made hard riding. I had been going for about an hour when suddenly, as I came down the far side of a gentle undulation, there was an explosion beneath me: the back tyre bursting.

This was very disappointing. I'd have to walk back to Escara and leave the bicycle. I wouldn't be able to reach Chipayas tonight. There was no point wheeling it all the way there.

Unless I hid it. Who would find it out here on this scrubby plain? I'd be back for it in a few days' time. So I buried it under shrubs and tussocks, taking my bearings from two blue mountains on the horizon and an old stone corral a mile away. I also sprinkled handfuls of dust over it. I thought this might diminish the chance of it flashing in sunlight to a passerby.

I walked on. Raised mounds had been swept clean of shrubs and had become sand dunes, a foreboding of what will in time happen to the rest of the plain. Over in the west the volcanoes along the Chilean border glinted white above the nearer ridges. The plain was frightening: the sand dunes were the first sign that the malignant disease of drought was terminal; this land was being parched to the bone, into a desert. Against the dark hills, ghouls of dust spiralled up in the wind and came spinning towards me, past me; departing spirits.

I came to the Lauca again, here only shin-deep and covering not half of its wide bed. The shrubs thinned out. Shells of adobe houses stood here and there, all of them round Uru-style houses. Probably they had been deserted thirty years ago when the township of Chipaya was founded, a last attempt to consolidate the dispersed tribe.

Then a Chipaya came past on a bicycle. He was wearing a dirty grey and brown smock tied round the middle with a rope. He stopped to talk to me, grinning continually. He said how near I was to Chipaya, pointing to a tiny stick against a mountain blue in the distance. It was the church tower of Chipaya.

With the sun about to set and the wind at its strongest, I reached the town. Four men in smocks with ropes round the middle like friars silently led me to a house on the square. We all waited outside, the wind strong on our faces. Soon a small man came across the square, dressed as the others. Without a word to anyone, like a teacher arriving, the man unlocked the door and went inside leaving the door open. Then he called something out and we all shuffled inside.

The man sat behind a table. He had a big book open in front of him. There was still enough light in the window for him to write by. He was the Corregidor. He wanted my passport. He had a small, unfriendly face and he slapped my passport on to the table impatiently, like a bureaucrat. Very slowly, with satisfaction, he copied my details into the book, smacking his lips on completion of each line. He was writing an Act authorizing my stay in Chipaya.

'Do you want a photograph permit?' he asked, not looking up.

'What?'

'A photograph permit. A hundred and fifty pesos.' That was twenty dollars.

'What for?'

'To take photographs. It's illegal to take pictures in Chipaya. Only with the special permit.'

The other four nodded gravely.

'And fifty pesos for the Act,' added the Corregidor.

'What is the Act?' I enquired as politely as I could.

The Corregidor looked up, his small, leathery monkey face scowling. 'Without an Act you cannot stay in Chipaya,' he snapped, then smacked his lips.

'Sí, sí,' mumbled the others in the room.

'Bueno,' I said, pulling out money.

'And I will lodge you myself,' said the Corregidor.

Was the lodging included in the price of the Act? I didn't dare ask then.

He took me to his compound and gave me a small hut to sleep in, one of the few square homes in Chipaya. It was filled with sheepskins and old beer crates.

The Chipayas are a decaying tribe. They will soon disappear like the rest of the Urus. Their land is drying up now. The concrete houses of the plaza are already crumbling in the fierce wind. Around the square stand the circular adobe huts with their shallow cones of thatch, like Chinese hats. When they came in from their lonely homes scattered over the plain to this even lonelier town, they gave up what little agriculture they used to maintain, except for a few scrawny potato patches. Only the government rice they are given keeps them alive; but it has also killed their will to fend for themselves. After centuries of ill-treatment they are defenceless against assistance. Like animals in a zoo, they are kept.

All day the men sit around the village doing nothing. They wander in and out of the one shop chatting and buying nothing. Occasionally they pick potatoes. Often they gather to mend a bicycle. They still wear their filthy striped smocks and hang their jaws open to breathe enough of the thin air, but within they are no longer Chipayas: their spirits are broken. Unless, of course, they are still just the stupid, listless people that the Aymaras say they have always been.

Chipaya women wear robes and shawls of brown sackcloth which they weave themselves. Under their shawls their hair is plaited into hundreds of tiny plaits hanging down in rows. Very occasionally they wash their hair. This they do in their own urine. Given time, human urine ferments into a strong disinfectant like ammonia.

And all day long the women sit outside the mud huts in their family yards. Mainly they cook and prepare food. They grind chunks of salt between stones and stand great pots of water to boil over small fires. There are little walls of mud surrounding the fire for the pot to stand on. The walls have holes to allow air in and fresh fuel. The women are very thrifty with firewood. The only wood they have is the thin, twisted kenoa tree, and a small, knotted root that burns. They keep an orange flame going in the middle of the fireplace and poke branches in through the holes, feeding them further in as they burn down. As the clay of the little supporting walls heats up it takes only a candle-size flame and a heart of embers to keep a great cauldron of water on the boil.

All the children from five to eleven years old go to the school, a concrete building that occupies one side of the square. But the teachers, outsiders, are underpaid and ineffective: few of the pupils can speak, let alone read or write, anything other than the native *poquina*. Nor do they need to. Chipaya is too isolated and distant to play an active part in the life of the nation.

In the middle of April, when I was there, they hold a fiesta to celebrate the founding of the town. The Corregidor and his few officials would march around the town bearing Bolivian flags with a small brass band following, and then return to the square to give ferociously patriotic speeches by the flagpole. The natives all looked on mutely, ready to shout 'Viva!' whenever called to. The whole village constituted only a meagre crowd on one side of the square. They were dumb spectators to this absurd ceremony in which the Corregidor, a small drunk man, attempted to express the Chipayas' importance for Bolivia: as the oldest of its peoples they had a crucial role to play in the nationhood. When he had woken me that morning he had come in and saluted, tottering about still blind drunk from the night before. He had latched on to the significance of the Chipayas as the last of their kind, and took it as an excuse for ridiculously pompous and patriotic beliefs about Bolivia. So he would shout out, 'Viva Bolivia!' and 'Viva General García Meza!' to the crowd in the square, and they would shout back 'Viva!' without knowing what they were referring to. For them the fiesta was beer and music: they were glad to hear the band rather than the wind in the square. It was not until a small group of sampoña-pipe players trooped out that they suddenly came to life. Sampoña are Pan pipes. A ring of Chipayas spontaneously formed to dance round the players in a slow trudging dance, stepping down heavily into the earth. The sad but lively music touched them. They understood it. For a moment they regained their vigour, their own culture, and seemed living Chipayas.

But then the Corregidor and his band marched around the plaza once more and the Chipayas fell back into listless spectatorship. The speeches resumed, and the martial tunes.

The following day I wanted to leave. But the Corregidor would not let me go until I had paid him double what we had agreed beforehand. He was still drunk. He tapped a pencil on a scrap of paper and wrote out some figures and rapping the paper with the lead again he announced my bill, his eyes swimming and bloodshot, shining even in the dark room. I said surely it wasn't that much. He said he would radio ahead to Escara and have me arrested if I didn't pay at once. He would not listen to me. He was stubborn like a child, pouting his lips then looking away with the furious determined look of a boy playing at soldiers.

My patience eroded, I gave him the sum originally agreed and left him staring into his palm, too drunk and lazy to lift his other hand to count the coins. I went past the football pitch where bicycles stood upended on their saddles. Men squatting at them stopped their tinkering to watch me draw away. They all shouted and raised their arms angrily when I took parting photographs of them, but I took them anyway.

An American businessman is negotiating a deal with the Bolivian government to export the Chipayas en masse to Arizona. He will set them up in a replica traditional village as a tourist attraction, the last of the Urus.

By the time I finished the walk to Escara it was night. One shop in the main square was open. The rest of the plaza was frozen into immobility by the moon, and the church was white and intricate like icing. Boulders and their shadows crowded a hill above the houses, making a tapestry of black and white.

Xavier welcomed me into his house. The bicycle had still been where I hid it, which was such a relief that the puncture of the back tyre seemed a trifle. But Xavier took this very gravely. He knelt down and examined the wheel.

'How did it happen?'

'It just burst. It was very weak. You see, where he wrapped it up.'

'I don't know,' Xavier shook his head. 'I don't know what he'll say.'

The uncle lived next door. He wheeled the bicycle into his yard with a grateful smile. I told him about the tyre. He smiled, nodded, thanked me for returning the bike; he hardly seemed to understand. If he did, he didn't mind at all.

Xavier's mother gave me a bowl of stew—yellow water with a couple of twists of stomach lining. His father watched quietly in darkness as I drank and tried to eat. He was suspicious about his brother's bicycle tyre.

In the morning all the inhabitants of Escara crammed into a convoy of three lorries to rattle along to Huachacalla, the next village down the road to Oruro, away from Chile. The President of Bolivia was meant to be visiting the barracks at Huachacalla that day. Some of the men were already drunk, and the most noticeably so, a man from whom I had at first tried to hire a bicycle for the journey to Chipaya, suddenly fell against me as the lorry jounced over a bump. He looked at me blankly.

'Do you want a bicycle?' he asked.

'No.'

'I've got six bicycles.'

'But I don't want one.'

'A hundred dollars.'

'What?'

'You can hire one for a hundred dollars.'

'A hundred dollars?' I laughed.

'Sí.'

He was spitting over me as he spoke, which I asked him not to do. He turned away and called something to another man.

I made to sit down, but there wasn't room so I had to squat. The whole lorry was excited, everyone laughing and shouting. At the front a man was holding two rolled-up Bolivian flags and a banner saying 'Escara greets General Meza'. A woman sitting next to me was carefully putting coca leaves between her rubbery lips. When a sudden jolt knocked me back against the side of the lorry, she smiled at me and patted my leg. She gave me some coca leaves and a tiny piece of *lejia*, the grey lime which they eat with coca to release the active alkali in the leaves. This was the first time a Chola woman showed me any special kindness. She had seen me hurt.

As soon as the villagers climbed out of the lorry at Huachacalla they were lost in the crowds of Cholos. Arches had been erected all the way up a street to the plaza. They were made of wood and wire and had been wrapped in blankets and hung with feathers and spoons, a traditional Uru ornament. The reds and yellows and blues and greens of the blankets on these structures rose above the crowd, which was itself a seething mass of primary colours. Each arch was the pride of a family or community, who would be gathered in a dense throng under it, dressed as if to outdo their creation in brilliance. They wanted to sate the eye, these Cholos; for a day to combat and defeat the bland suede tone of the Altiplano. There were musicians too at many arches: flute players and drummers dressed up like birds of paradise with dyed feathers sprouting from their shoulders and heads and hanging down the back in long Red Indian headdresses. As they played they would dance, stomping and hopping to the beat of the drums. And since the arches were less than twenty yards apart the tune of each band had to be piped and thumped all the louder to smother the competition. But it didn't matter how many groups played, how many melodies intertwined themselves: the more music, the merrier are the Cholos. It is the music above all that frees their spirits: it drowns the noise of the wind.

I needed to find some breakfast, so I left the throng for a quiet side street of tin-roofed adobe homes. Here the village was peaceful, though anticipation hung in the air. I came to an open doorway; the nearest thing to a shop or restaurant sign. Inside was a bare room, with a table and two benches. An army officer, a young well-built man with a moustache, was eating boiled eggs with a young woman who was thickly made up and smartly dressed. She was no Indian: she was a white Bolivian like him. She looked wealthy too; she had probably come from La Paz. So this officer must be her husband or fiancé or boyfriend.

'Buenos días,' they both said with welcoming smiles as I came in. The officer graciously invited me to sit with a gesture of his hand. The girl beamed, unless it was her make-up shining.

'Where are you from?' she asked, half-cocking her head. Hopefully: 'California?' (Wealthy South Americans love to be associated with their northern neighbours, both socially and in the estimation of the world: they feel they deserve to be, considering how they emulate the American dream in the suburbs of their capitals.)

'Inglaterra,' I disappointed her.

But no, her face lit up. So did the young officer's.

'Sí?' he asked. 'A beautiful country, no?'

'Not as beautiful as Bolivia,' I said.

He grimaced; then thought somehow I might be offended, and said: 'You think so?'

'Of course.'

The girl said: 'Me, I like Europe. I like cities . . . Have you been to La Paz?'

'Not yet.'

'It's lovely. Well, compared to here it's lovely. I'm only here for the ceremony.'

'What ceremony?'

'The ceremony in the barracks,' answered the officer with a polite smile. 'With the President.'

I said: 'So the President really is coming?'

'General T. García Meza,' confirmed the officer.

The girl was still smiling: to meet a European, an Englishman, in Huachacalla. You never knew when you would get lucky.

The Chola woman who ran this pension brought me boiled eggs too. When I went back out into the fiesta the street up to the square had become a great canal of dancing. At every arch rings of women plodded round and round, most of them Cholas, some, from small *comunidades*, Quechuas in black dresses with golden, red and yellow embroidery round the hem. They cried out and whooped and grinned as they danced, and the musicians, who were all men, all but laughed into their flutes. Drums were beaten so hard they lost their resonance; they sounded like metal trays being banged. But so much the better; their rhythm was loud and strong. It infested everyone now. Even old men were stepping about with beer bottles in their hands.

Then the sound of an aeroplane droned through the din, and a small plane swooped low over the town and circled. Like a sudden appearance of the Spirit of God, it doubled the fervour of the celebration. The sight of an aeroplane was in itself a rare cause for celebration; but this one was carrying the President of Bolivia, without doubt the most important man in the world, even if he was apt to change his name every few months. Perhaps that was an aspect of his importance. Everywhere bottles of beer were being opened and passed round, and new crates were being carried out into the street. A few minutes later news that the President had been driven from the aeroplane to the army barracks in a jeep filtered up the street, and all the people streamed off to the barracks in one surge. The line of arches was suddenly deserted, blazing silently in the sun.

The ceremony in the barracks was long and boring: there were endless presentations of certificates, and unimpressive displays of gymnastics and athletics. The Cholos all stood around in a great square, obediently watching, waiting for the moment when the President would walk up to the plaza. They realized it had come, the ceremony was over: they ran back out into the street in a great stampede to take up positions around their arches again: desperately all the bands started playing their pipes, while the women freed bags of confetti from the folds of their dresses. In a moment the street was again thick with people and music.

The President began his walk up to the square with a brass band blasting out a march right behind him. As he passed under the first arch two women thrust a long poncho over his head. His cap fell off and he bent down to pick it up. Before he could put it on again the women had stuck an Aymara hat on his head too, a woollen hat with long earflaps. He forced a smile and nodded thanks, his cap in his hand. Great dignitaries don't expect a complete foreigner to join in their fiesta. They wanted an Indian prince, not a general.

All the way up the street was a long way: the Cholos made no gangway for his procession. One after another men shook his hand and women gathered round to shower him with confetti. A band of pipe-players managed to get between the President and the military band. The ceremony was transformed by the crowd into a welcome an Inca noble might have been given.

The President of Bolivia tolerated it: the crowd obviously intended no disrespect, though it ignored formalities customary to him.

When he finally reached the square he climbed up on to a platform, careful not to trip on his poncho, to give a speech. He spoke in Spanish of the marvellous welcome, and how overwhelmingly friendly they had been; and then about the hand-ploughs the government had donated to the area, and how excellent the regiment was. The Cholos listened eagerly for a while, and then gradually dispersed into shops to drink beer and play pipes and dance. For a moment the reason for their fiesta had entered it and been a part of it. But it had stepped out again, on to the rostrum; while they were still here to celebrate. They would carry on until night when lorries would take them back to their tedious lives, from which they would not break free till the next fiesta. These hours were too precious to waste: not even the President could keep them from the drink and the dance.

As I stood watching the President in the square, taking the

odd photograph, I heard a voice behind say, 'Venga!' Come! The command was repeated several times. Then the voice said: 'Eh! Gringo, venga!'

At this I turned: a deeply tanned white Bolivian was staring straight at me.

'Security,' he said. 'You can't take pictures here. Come with me.' He was talking quietly, almost smiling too. 'Come. Now.'

I thought maybe if I just ignored him he would go away. I turned back to the rostrum. I couldn't quite believe him.

But he persisted. 'Venga, gringo. Venga! Ahora!'

I was half-heartedly strolling away, vaguely under the pretext of not understanding Spanish; he called out 'Stop!', which is international; I turned round, and saw how earnest he was: he was pointing an enormous revolver at me.

By now I had put my camera away.

'Camera,' said the man.

'What?'

'Las fotos,' the man urged. 'La película.' The film. He beckoned with his free hand.

'What?'

'Las fotos.'

But an air of unreality lingered.

'Ahora!' he ordered.

I began opening my camera bag.

'No!' cried the man, nervous. 'Vámonos.' Let's go.

He made me walk to the barracks, driving me down with the gun pointing at my back.

At the gate, where he felt safer and I anxious not to be taken any further, he again demanded the camera. I asked why once, and then handed over a film canister saying, 'But there's nothing. Nada. No pictures of here.' He put away his gun and disappeared inside.

I was standing there stunned when the officer with whom I had breakfasted arrived. He greeted me effusively, hoping to consolidate a friendship with a westerner. And here was a perfect opportunity. For I told him at once what had happened.

He looked at his boots; then lifted his face to say: 'Leave it to me.'

While I waited for him his girlfriend or wife arrived. 'Qué tal?' she greeted me.

I told her my big problem, because she might bring pressure to bear on her boyfriend if he failed to recover the film at the first attempt.

But a moment later he reappeared and proudly handed over the wrongly seized article, raising his hand to forestall my thanks: all he needed was my address, because he was hoping to come to Europe next year.

He didn't know that he had just done his President a disservice.

5

AYMARAS

THE Aymaras are the main Indian group of the Altiplano, though they are scarcely a group: any Indian whose native language is Aymara is an Aymara. Only back in the pre-Inca days when the Aymaras held the great empire of Tiahuanaco did they constitute a cultural unit. After its fall they disintegrated into twelve mutually hostile kingdoms. In the fifteenth century the Incas won the allegiance of all twelve. Since the Spanish Conquest the Aymaras have dissipated still further into isolated and unfriendly communities who share only a language and certain customs.

In the last decade, however, an Aymara independence movement has emerged. In their manifesto they claim that the Aymara people wish to be independent of the postcolonial yoke; that the Altiplano always has been and always must be an independent Aymara territory; that the Aymaras have the oldest and therefore most valid claim to the Altiplano. (These idealists overlook the older Urus.) But the far-sighted movement has yet to spread from the common rooms of the University of La Paz. The Aymara villagers are ignorant of the work of liberation undertaken on their behalf. They continue to be born into traditional lives in remote communities where little has changed since the collapse of the Tiahuanaco empire.

When an Aymara is born, a *yatiri*, a witch, tears off a piece of the afterbirth. He floats it in a bowl of water and studies it closely. Does it expand or contract? Does it drift to the side of the bowl and stay there? Which side? The answers to these questions determine whether the young Aymara will survive infancy, childhood and youth, and how best to encourage his survival.

For the witch must see in the bowl the *huaca* to which offerings shall be made for the baby. A huaca is a shrine, a spirit's dwelling place. A rock, a cave, a mountain, a spring, almost any feature of the land can be a huaca.

Then the yatiri buries the placenta in the floor of the house, by the door, along with a small, flint knife. He ties a thong with a little leather pouch containing salt, dried pepper and another very small flint knife round the infant's neck. Why does he do these things? To ward off evil spirits?

The little necklace has nothing to do with evil spirits. It's there to keep the baby's soul in the young body, where it belongs. Aymara souls all live in mountains and hills. Generally the mountain nearest a village, the most prominent nearby peak, is designated as the home of the souls, a soul-storehouse. When a baby is born a soul is sent out from this mountain to take up the new vacancy. The trouble is, souls don't like leaving their mountain for a human frame. They are creatures of habit, by nature sedentary. Yet they must go. Pacha Mama, the Earth Mother, won't let them stay. But once in the young body they will do all they can to escape. This is why the witch ties the thong round the neck: it acts as a barrier to keep the soul in. And when death comes the converse problem arises: the soul has now grown accustomed to its home in the body, and doesn't want to leave that. So a rope is tied round the neck of the corpse, this time to keep the evicted soul out. The Aymaras feel that although it is hard to come into this life, it is equally hard to leave it: their philosophy is in the end optimistic.

But why the salt and chili pepper in the little pouch of the necklace? These are the best condiments the Aymaras have: they are offered to the newly arrived soul to coax it into staying, to show it that life won't be so bad in its new home. And the little flint knife?

The knife stakes a claim. It shows the soul that this is indeed its patch. Like the knife stuck in the floor, which is the most crucial measure: it marks irrefutably where the baby belongs, in this house. And the soul, with its knife, belongs in this baby. (When Manco Capac, the mythical ancestor of the Incas, was sent forth to found their capital Cuzco, he knew only that the city must be where the golden dagger he had been given fell into the ground of its own accord.)

So why is the placenta buried too? Partly to mark the home of the child; partly to thank the earth that yielded up the new life, to return to the earth a token of what it gave. For in Aymara science every life form, whether a dog or a potato, is born of the earth. Conception and pregnancy, of which the Aymaras are well aware, are but the physical counterparts of the real process. What is a body without a soul? Dead. The important thing, the life, is the soul. And that comes from Pacha Mama, from the earth. It's only natural to thank her for her gift. But there is another reason.

Pacha Mama, though omnipresent, is not immortal. She is a living thing, and must be kept alive. She must be fed. How can the earth go on feeding people and yielding up new life indefinitely if it never gets anything in return? Obviously you have to give it suitable food: alcohol, coca leaves, bread, fat, blood, placenta, a llama foetus. This is why the witch must know where the baby's huaca is to be. The huaca is the place where Pacha Mama will be fed on behalf of the new human life.

Aymaras believe that the earth needs them to survive just as much as they need it. The two feed each other. This symbiotic relationship underlies all Aymara life; in fact, all Andean life. When Aymaras were forced to work in mines, to dig out the very flesh of their Pacha Mama, they were driven to worship of the Christian devil.

Before the Spanish Conquest shaft mining was unknown in the Andes. Pre-Columbian ore was quarried or panned from the rivers. Offerings were made to Pacha Mama for all that was taken. The brilliant stones were deposited by the celestial bodies as they laboured through her bowels every twelve or thirteen hours to reach the east where they would soar into the sky again. Gold was the sun's sweat. Silver was the moon's tears.

The Spaniards made the Indians excavate far greater quantities of ore than they had ever known before. One night an old devil was spotted on the hills above the mines. Hahuari was leading a llama train down into the earth. The beasts were laden with ore. So it was the old devil who was bringing the tons of ore into the mines. Instead of making offerings to Pacha Mama, then, it was Hahuari who deserved the gifts. So figures of this devil were carved at whose feet little sacrifices could be made. And what did he look like? He had horns, a tail, an erect penis, and he carried a pitchfork. He was the very devil the missionaries had warned the Indians of.

Why did the miners make Hahuari look like the Devil? Because they decided that was who he must be. There was one big difference between all the work they had done before the Spaniards came and the kind of work they did after. They made their offerings as before and were given ore in exchange. But in front of their very eyes the ore was whisked away by the owners of the mine once it reached the shaft mouth. It was given to them yet it didn't belong to them. What kind of an exchange was that? Something only a foreign devil could be party to.

Which is why to this day the Aymara tin miners of Bolivia

spend their wages as fast and as recklessly as they can: get rid of them, they're the wages of the Devil.

Pacha Mama isn't the only divine being the Aymaras know. In fact the Aymara world is pregnant with spirits, quite apart from the great rolling womb they plough.

One of the most important deities is Tunupa, the thunder god. He is responsible for sending hail, the greatest misfortune that can befall the Aymaras. On the Altiplano hail comes like a rain of pebbles. In half an hour it pummels the crops to shreds and stones the baby llamas to death. The only people who can appeal to Tunupa are the witches. They have a special relationship with him, for the only way to become a witch is to be struck by lightning. A man must be struck twice. The first bolt shatters his being; the second reconstitutes him as a witch. It always happens on a lonely mountain, far from the sight of any other men. Then he returns to the village and says: 'Now I know,' and his apprenticeship to an old witch begins. Tunupa sends the lightning bolts.

I took a night bus from Huachacalla back to Oruro, the first Bolivian bus I travelled in. After all the open lorries it was a nightmare, crowded and very hot, even in the freezing night, as if the axles and drive-shaft were generating tremendous heat under the floor. Meanwhile I had conceived an army of frantic bacteria who made my stomach swell and ache. My forehead had become as hot as a branding iron. And I had no seat. I had been assigned one of the beer crates in the gangway for a place when I had bought my ticket, but there were so many standing passengers by the time I boarded—and even men grinning in the luggage racks—that I decided to slump on the steps by the door.

When the bus stopped for the curfew, by the raftsmen's ragged camp on the bank of the Río Lauca, all the passengers climbed out while I lay where I was, too ill to move. One after another the women's skirts brushed over my face. The stench was horrifying: they never have baths. I almost retched.

But the bacteria moved on rapidly: by the time I reached

Oruro they had evacuated my frame and my fever had died down.

The next night I met Gonzalo Lazaro in the chic bar-restaurant.

'Interst? . . . aha . . .' he asked.

'Yes. Very.' I told him about the fiesta in Huachacalla.

'You have bery lucky,' he said.

His jeep was fixed. We would leave next day to visit remote Aymara communities.

The eastern half of the Altiplano is composed of dry, smooth mountains. The flat plain which stretches from the Western Cordillera is suddenly crumpled and thrown up in barren hills, like lumps pushing up under a carpet. This eastern Puna used to be the realm of the Charcas, one of the most powerful Aymara groups, and it is still an Aymara stronghold where life goes on unchanged. Our destination was Sacaca, the Charcas' old capital, now a small, unimportant town.

We left Oruro in the morning in Gonzalo's jeep. The track headed due east, straight and flat, until the early afternoon. Then we reached the hills which had lain sunbathing on the horizon all morning. Suddenly we were climbing, skirting hillsides, traversing valleys, coming over barren brows.

We made slow progress. The track was in very poor condition, Gonzalo said, though it looked like any other to me.

Gonzalo had plenty of time to talk about the Indians. He would begin his sentence with at most a single word and then stave off my attempts to prompt him by saying, 'Er . . . er . . . er.' He wouldn't acknowledge that we both spoke good Spanish. But when he did finally complete a simple sentence of English such as: 'Aymaras . . . er . . . er . . . less olt . . . ze Urus,' he turned to smile so triumphantly, often breaking out in glorious laughter, that it was worth the wait.

The Aymaras have a reputation for aggressiveness, he explained. They used to hold an empire and to be warriors. They have always been recalcitrant. The Incas succeeded in subduing most of them, but only indirectly through their kings and leaders, who were won over by bribes or threats into

The school concert near Sacaca

The President and aides at the Huachacalla fiesta

Aymaras at the tinku fiesta in Bolívar

(*Top*) Quechua boy

(*Above*) Breakfast in the Cordillera Vilcanota

(*Right*) Aymara boy

The eastern Altiplano

Tinku fight at Bolivar

Llica, by the Salar de Uyuni

Huachacalla fiesta

Chola women at the market in Oruro

Raqchi dance fiesta

The cemetery at Chipaya

(*Left*) Salinas de García Mendoza, near the sh●
of the Salar de Uyuni

(*Below*) The Inca at the Inti Raymi festival
in Cuzco

compliance with the Cuzco administration. Once the Inca dynasty ended, in the late sixteenth century, the Spaniards never managed to incorporate all the Aymaras in the Viceroyalty of Upper Peru, nor since Republican times has Bolivia. There are Aymara miners, of course, and most of the Cholos are former Aymaras. But there are still thousands of Indians living out in the hills of this eastern Puna who play no part in the Bolivian nation. Gonzalo's arrival among them as representative of the Institute for Agricultural Transformation was something quite novel: never before have they been offered help and advice from outside about where to plant what, nor do they welcome it. They're devoted to the ancient monotony of their lives.

Dusk was gathering and we still hadn't reached the first town we were to pass, Bolívar, so named because when a corporal of the Republican forces spent a night there the deeply awed Indians believed him to be the great liberator Simón Bolívar himself, and repaid the honour of his visit by renaming their village. Then, under the late sky, we saw a group of Aymaras plodding along the crest of a hill. Below them were two steep square fields patched on the hillside. They were a forlorn-looking troupe, five men in large hats carrying their ploughshares and digging-sticks across the slouching back of the hill.

'Papas, papas, siempre papas,' Gonzalo complained, glancing over at the fields. 'Only . . . only . . . er . . . eat . . . er . . .'

'Potat—' I ventured.

'Er,' he insisted, 'er . . . potito,' and he laughed out loud.

Night was fast approaching when we finally bounced into Bolívar. All along the walls of the dark-glowing adobe houses stood shadowy figures, all with large-brimmed white felt hats pulled low over their foreheads. Their eyes shone beneath, out of the swarthiness of their faces. They turned to watch as we rocked past.

Gonzalo said, 'You have lucky.' There was a fiesta going on. Otherwise the streets would be empty.

Here and there a door stood open and cast a rectangle of

yellow light on to the track: shops, open till late tonight. Though the town wasn't crowded there were figures outside every house, at every corner.

Gonzalo muttered curses when the Indians were too slow in getting out of our way. He was nervous because when they drink as they do at fiestas Indians are unpredictable. Some of the men had broad, fixed grins shining white at us. Others seemed to make a show of ignoring us, turning their backs deliberately. Some laughed loudly.

We parked by the new concrete schoolroom of Bolívar, where we would eat supper and spend the night.

I walked down into town with Gonzalo to buy food while the schoolteacher guarded the jeep. Night had fallen by now and the charanga-players had started up. Charangas are tiny mandolins made of armadillo shells. Several men were listlessly strumming out chords while dancing groups formed, wide circles of twenty or thirty men and women who trudged slowly round and round.

We went into the nearest store. It was just an adobe room with a wooden counter and shelves of tins. By the door stood sacks of rice and flour and sugar and pink square cans of paraffin. The shopkeeper, an old Cholo in a grey suit, was pouring from one of these cans into a little glass bottle like a medicine bottle. Three Aymaras stood waiting.

In the light of a fierce paraffin lamp they were an impressive sight. Outside in the night the brilliance of the Aymaras' clothes didn't show. They were wearing short woollen trousers like culottes which were either black or white, and dusty, with heavy bands of gold embroidery around the hems. Then waistcoats of strong colours: red, green, blue, yellow, in check designs, or simply with a pattern of black lines criss-crossing the solid colour. And then jerkins, short jackets, very tight, of the same brilliance as the waistcoats but never the same hue. Their collars were turned up scruffily. On top, the white felt hats favoured by Aymaras of the Puna, large, wide, almost conical hats that shade the face. Two men wore typical Andean hats, tall woollen ones with long earflaps, underneath their white felt ones, for warmth and for show: the earflaps were colourful and hung down almost to the shoulders. In the glare of the artificial light the men's garments were startling. The three of them stood in an obedient line waiting for their drink.

When the bottle was handed over one of the men tucked it into the waistband of his trousers. Another pulled out his own bottle as they stepped outside. I saw him pour a splash on to the ground, mumble something and then take a long swig. Each of his friends did the same as the bottle was passed round. They were making their libations to Pacha Mama. They disappeared into the drunken fiesta.

'They drink paraffin?' I asked Gonzalo.

'No. It's alcohol,' he said. 'But pure, pure, pure. A hundred per cent.'

The storekeeper had a bunch of bananas on the counter. The tropical valleys on the edge of the Amazon lowlands were less than two days' walk away, even though Bolívar was at 15,000 feet on the barren Puna. We bought sardines, crackers and bananas for supper. There was no bread in Bolívar, but our meal was already a feast. Most of the Aymaras of this region live on potatoes alone.

Afterwards Gonzalo wanted to take me to meet his friend the Padre. But he was unsure about walking, especially with a gringo in tow. On the other hand the jeep would attract so much more attention.

We took the jeep anyway. The street seemed more crowded now. It had the atmosphere of the edge of a funfair, where everyone is walking about in small groups, not thronged together but making their way to the central hive. There were many women too who wore thick black dresses with gold and red embroidery at the hem and across the breast. They had felt hats like the men. Some of them wore wool socks. Most went in only sandals.

We had to pass two dancing groups, circles of plodding people that stretched right across the way. They would stop trudging round as we drove near, glance into the headlights and fall apart to either side of the road. As we moved past, the thin, delicate chords of the charangas became audible, almost a sad sound, a feeble plinking. Armadillo shells don't make resonant sound-boxes, but they do produce clear, tuneful notes. The men playing would grin fixedly and carry on shuffling their feet in time. They held their instruments high, without a strap, and strummed lightly with an easy rhythm using all their fingers.

Bolívar was a *pueblo*, a little town, so it had a plaza. All the Aymaras had come in for the fiesta from their *comunidades*, their communities out in the hills. But the plaza, when we finally rolled into it, was almost empty. There were just a few men drinking along one wall. It was no more than a rocky space among the dwellings, not even square. It sloped away steeply. Up above, on a rise of the land on the far side, stood the church, small and pale.

We pulled up beside a bush below the church. A path marked out by pebbles led to a concrete house with a glass door. A paraffin lamp burned within. This was the Padre's house.

He was a large man with short white hair and a sun-creased face. He greeted us as if we had only been gone an hour and had business to get down to. We all sat in the kitchen, which was also the living room.

The Padre was a Spaniard. He had been in Bolivia seventeen years now and he would never come to understand the Bolivians. He just couldn't get his message across. 'Why did they come in for this fiesta?' he asked. 'Why? They say it was for a little fair, an animal fair. Maybe five alpacas were bought and sold. Maybe some chickens too. But they'll be here for a whole week. Five more days. And what do they do? They drink. That's all they do. They just drink, nothing more. And they fight, of course.'

Gonzalo turned to me: 'You'll see the *tinku* tomorrow. Very interesting.'

'Drinking and fighting,' the Padre said, 'drinking and fighting. But why? Why? Or when they come in for a funeral they all run into the cemetery in a great multitude, as fast as they can. You know why? It's because they're all afraid of being the last one into the graveyard. The last one is the next one to die. Yes, the next to die. Then all the children have to leap over the grave before it is filled in. Why? It makes them strong. It means they'll live to be adults.

'You see? Why do they believe all this? Why? And when they drink, always Pacha Mama, Pacha Mama. Pacha Mama has to drink too. They think Pacha Mama is thirsty. Why? Who knows? No one can say why. It's just custom, that's all. Custom. *Es la costumbre.'*

The Padre looked at me, his eyes hard brown, and glanced at the window. He had no more to say. Since we had come to see these very customs, we weren't the allies we might have been.

In the morning, over the dust of the square, two men stomp towards one another. They are swinging their arms and stooping forwards like apes. Now the morning sun has just become warm and the Aymaras have been drinking pure alcohol. The time is right for tinku.

The two men, still ape-swinging their arms, are staring at one another with hateful eyes. They are close together now. Suddenly one wildly swings an arm out at the other and his fist connects on the chin. The man's head is jolted back and his big white hat is sent flying by the force of the blow. But he's not swayed; immediately he strikes back with a long-swinging fist that hits on the temple, knocking the other's head to the side. Their mouths are open in anger as blow after blow knocks them, making their thick black mops of hair flop about the skull. One kicks straight-legged and hard with his heavy boot. He hits the knee. The other is furious, throws himself forwards, both arms outstretched on to the kicker's shoulders, pushing him with the whole force of his anger and weight, forcing him backwards so violently that the man stumbles and falls on to the ground with the pusher on top of him. At once the schoolteacher is at them with the cane, until they come apart and stand and retreat into the crowd. Already two other men have stepped out into the ring formed by the watching people and are ape-swinging their arms at each other.

The rule is, you have to stop when a man is down. No one can stand two rounds, either. Once the fight is over both have to leave the ring. They used to be fights to the death, says Gonzalo, with weapons. The losers used to get eaten by the winner and his family.

Now the second pair are smashing at each other's heads. The first pair are somewhere in the circle of blazingly-coloured jackets and waistcoats. One of them was given his hat back by someone in the crowd. He had blood on his swarthy cheek and one of his eyes was swollen up into a ball.

This morning, before the tinku began, the Padre insisted that every man carry a rock up to the cemetery and add it to the wall he was having built there. All the Aymaras grinned as they slogged up the hill leaning forwards and carrying the stones behind their backs. In Inca times it was a punishment to have to go around with a rock like that all day. The Padre didn't know this, though. He just wanted to get something out of them before they fell into their violent ways.

It's only in the morning, for the tinku, that the Aymaras congregate in the plaza. Apart from the circular throng with the open ring in the middle there are several other groups and clusters of people. Two dancing rings have formed, charangas plinking away. They may be members of other communities waiting for their turn in the tinku. There are many women standing loose in the square, very few in the central crowd of spectators. Sometimes women will attack one another, though it isn't customary like the men's fighting. One woman just ran shrieking from her enemy who had clawed her below the neck, to the water trough standing in the middle of the square, and leaned forwards pulling her black dress away from her breast to splash water on her wound, gasping and crying with rage.

A third pair is already smashing out at one another. Then

they each grab the other's arms and hold on like a pair of crabs claw to claw. One is in a brilliant blue jerkin, his head cropped round the sides so he has a thick shining mop on top that flicks from back to front and ear to ear. He is panting earnestly like a runner, mouth agape. His opponent is in yellow. He too has lost his hat. They shuffle round and round. Suddenly in a single movement the one in blue tugs the other close and delivers a cracking head-butt. The other kicks out but is pushed backwards as he does so and loses his balance, falling to the ground with the head-butter straddling him down.

Why do they fight? Fiestas are the only time they break free of the monotony of agricultural life to enjoy themselves. Their lives are like the blankets which the women weave: so much black suddenly broken here and there by strips of flaming colour, the fiestas where they drink and dance and play. So why smash each other up?

The fights are always between people from different communities; perhaps there is some natural hostility, and they fight like fans of opposing football teams. But the fighting is an integral part of the celebration. Every morning at every fiesta the men form a ring and the tinku begins. The fights aren't spontaneous outbursts of drunken excitement. They are a ritual. Perhaps, because the Aymaras have always been a warrior race, they need a dose of pure aggression every now and then. Tinku might exist simply for the sake of violence as an ingredient of life, as if it were uncontaminated here by personal involvement and were pure violence.

'In some places they still fight with weapons,' Gonzalo said. 'Sometimes they use stones which they hold in the hand. They suffer serious injuries in some villages.'

'Why?' I asked.

Back to English: 'It's . . . er . . . olt, olt. Bery olt.' He waved down his hand. 'A very ancient custom,' in Spanish.

We reached Sacaca in the late afternoon. It was a larger pueblo than Bolívar, having a wide square plaza fronted with low tin-roofed adobe houses. We stayed in a shop on the square, with a Chola woman who gave us supper at a little table by her door on the plaza. She stood quietly behind the counter as we ate; we heard her skirts rustling like a horse on straw. She watched us, whispering when an old man came in for rice.

Sacaca was a waste place, its ground parched like bone. The plaza was a desert hemmed in by the four low walls of houses. The church was crumbling. In the streets there were deep central gulleys like Roman drains. They were filled with refuse and dry dung and pebbles. The few inhabitants that could be seen, walking slowly across the square or resting in doorways, lived in the town like victims of its dry decay.

Except late at night, when the moon came up. Then into the blackness there rose a shining town and the ground of the plaza glowed. The drought was forgotten, the Altiplano was bathed in watery light and became a rich land with the friendly lamp above. It was only the sun which hurt the Altiplano. The moon nourished it.

In the morning we picked up Gonzalo's field assistant, an educated Aymara who spoke Spanish, and drove off to visit a small community out in the hills. We travelled high up on a huge valley side which reached arm upon long arm down into a dark ravine. Finally a steep llama trail, two mossy strips flanking a thin path of dust, brought us down to an open space above a small valley-bed. Below, tarnished golden roofs of straw caught the sunlight. A middle-aged man in Aymara dress came up to greet us. He smiled and shook our hands and spoke to the field assistant in Aymara. We followed down into the community.

It was a haphazard cluster of adobe dwellings. There were no streets. The houses stood in groups of two or three, compounds enclosed by low and often fallen walls of adobes. A little stream ran in deep banks through the village.

We passed through a gap in a wall. Beside it there was a house, ahead a large open ground gently sloping down to a tin-roofed building. This was the school in its playground.

Near the bottom of the slope sat a flock of black-haired children. Next to them were five empty chairs.

A man came out of the house by the gap to greet us. He was a white Bolivian, but thin like an Indian, with short greying hair and eyes tightened to the sun. He smiled and welcomed us in Spanish. He had been the schoolteacher here for three years, as long as there had been a school.

Two other Aymaras had joined us, village elders, so we were two chairs short. The teacher shouted at the pupils in Aymara, a guttural torrent, and four tiny urchins scampered off into the schoolroom and came out in pairs carrying a chair between them. The three Aymaras were already seated, not to miss the rare luxury of a chair. The teacher sat next to them with Gonzalo and the field assistant to his right, I on the end. We waited in the hot sun, a continual susurrus of whispers rising from the flock of pupils.

The teacher's assistant, a young Cholo in dirty slacks and a cardigan, came out in front with a cane. Without a word all the children rose and went to him, all perfect miniature Aymaras in waistcoats and jerkins and extra short trousers. Most were bareheaded. Some wore the *choro* hats, the typical Andean hats with earflaps. All wore sandals made out of tyre-treads strapped on with lengths of old inner tube. They were in their best, not barefoot today. They fell into a rough rectangle, the assistant between them and us, facing them, and they all began to sing, a thin chorus of hard voices, mechanical and not pretty.

They sang two songs in Aymara then one in Spanish, a flourish by the schoolteacher to impress the audience.

All the children went to sit down again. The assistant remained where he was. He beckoned with his cane. Three boys came back out. They climbed into a derelict house in front, a three-walled house open to us. It had a raised floor and two gaunt roof beams. It made a stage for the boys, who stood in a line looking over our heads and frowning in concentration once they began a long unison recitation. It was in Spanish, but incomprehensible. Even syllables were broken

97

in the middle by breaths, and few words escaped intact from the young throats. Their pronunciation was strange too, very forced. They were star pupils.

The two on either side stepped back. The teacher looked both ways along his audience and smiled as if to acknowledge our admiration, or to let us know we were in for something splendid now. The one boy in the middle remained at the front of the stage. He drew a deep breath and launched into song.

His voice was strong, the melody clear, the words just meaningless sounds. He had his eyes fixed on the far wall of the valley, his hands clenched by his sides. He drew his breaths so stiffly his body almost jumped each time. The choro hat he was wearing, too big for him, started tilting backwards and eventually fell back off his head. He carried on regardless. The two lads behind him looked at one another. As soon as the song ended and we all clapped, one of them whipped the hat off the floor and leaped roaring from the stage and hurled the thing into the crowd of schoolchildren, who broke into shouts and screams.

The schoolteacher turned either way to smile at us. The assistant with the cane took a bow and walked off. The two remaining boys stood stiffly where they were, eyes shining with excitement.

After this school concert the teacher took us up to his house by the gap in the wall. We sat at a table in a bare room. A large Chola woman, possibly his wife, waddled in and out with bowls of stew, in each bowl a heap of small potatoes, pink and yellow and white ones, with a twist of grey llama meat on top. We ate with spoons and had coffee afterwards. This was a feast.

Gonzalo and the teacher spoke about the Aymaras' diet. Then the teacher smiled at me: 'What did you think of the concert?'

'Fantastic.'

'Very intelligent, no? The children will grow up to be Castilian-speakers. It's very important. Very important.'

'To be Cholos?'

'To be Aymaras. Aymaras in the Bolivian nation.'

After lunch on our way back to the jeep Gonzalo's assistant led us into a family's compound where two women sat at a loom. He greeted them and they muttered a response without looking at him. They stopped their work and shuffled to their feet, eyes to the ground. Gonzalo told him to tell them to carry on. He did. They grew confused, standing to one side.

Their blanket was all black but for a trim they were weaving. It had motifs of a geometric camel-shaped animal, the old camel of the Andes which is now extinct, its brothers the llama, alpaca, vicuña and guanaco remaining. The design is at least two thousand years old.

Across on the other side of the yard a woman was squatting before a big flat rock on which she rolled a smooth stone back and forth, crushing salt from a hard cake into powder. She looked askance at us, mouth open, lips and teeth catching the sun. She was huddled in a black shawl over her black dress as she worked.

This was either the field assistant's family or else they were good friends of his. He lifted a wood board out of the way and led us crouching through a small doorway into the house.

It was almost pitch black at first. Then frayed light began to appear low down in the thatched roof and objects grew out of the darkness. It might have been a store room. Several sacks were stacked against one wall. There were sheepskins laid out on a slab of rock, but this was a bed. There were folded blankets, wooden tools, a small folding table, two paraffin cans. The earthen walls absorbed all sound, and all warmth. They would take in the heat of the sun in the day, keeping the interior cool, then breathe out the stored warmth at night. In this dark womb of mud one felt safe from the sun and the ice of the Altiplano.

From one of the thin roof beams hung two withered and knotted things, like old roots but shiny and gold-coloured. They were llama foetuses, dried in the sun and hanging there to protect those who lived within. They would bring fertility to the home: babies to the women, good crops to the fields. For a foetus is a very instance of fertility, of the continuation of life, which is the greatest preoccupation of the Aymaras. After the next harvest these things would be taken down and buried in a field, food for Pacha Mama, source of all fertility.

When we came out the women were back at their loom, their dresses brilliant black in the sunlight.

At the jeep the schoolteacher shook our hands and watched motionless as we rocked back up the llama trail, he alone again in that trough among the huge waves of the Altiplano, to continue his effort to civilize.

High on a mountainside we came across some Aymaras harvesting potatoes. We stopped and walked from the jeep towards a thin, dismal column of smoke. There was a small ashen fire smouldering in the corner of a field; around it sat a woman and three men. They bade us sit down while the woman rummaged among the ashes with a stick, to roll out several small potatoes. These she put on a little piece of cloth which she placed in front of us leaning over to open it out. The potatoes were grey from the fire, their thin skins peeling off. We were to dip them in a little metal bowl of sauce—salt and a grey mineral crushed into water. The mineral, like cement, made the mouth go dry. The salt made it water at the back. This sauce was a treat for the Aymaras. They sat there munching noisily, too absorbed in eating to speak, their digging sticks rested across their knees.

Later, on a wide flat hilltop a few miles from Sacaca, we rumbled past an old man trotting along our beaten track. He jumped on to the ladder at the back of the jeep as we bounced by, and clambered up on to the roof.

Gonzalo stopped and opened his window. 'Baja te,' he shouted. Get down.

The man stayed where he was, probably smiling into the distance.

'Baja te, baja te! Ahora!'

Gonzalo climbed out and stood away from his open door, looking at the roofrack. 'Baja te!' he shouted.

A whimpering, plaintive sound came from the roof.

'Baja te.'

There was silence.

'Baja te,' he appealed. 'Imposible. Peligroso.' Dangerous.

The man climbed down the ladder and stood on the bottom rung, his face just above the back window. I could see his dusty, sun-bleached waistcoat.

'Baja te,' Gonzalo insisted. 'Baja te.'

The man thought he'd be fine on the ladder, and stayed there.

'Ahora!' cried Gonzalo.

The man stepped to the ground, sun-blinded from the long afternoon.

Gonzalo said, 'Son animales,' as we drove on back to Sacaca.

The next morning a lorry driver happened to pass through Sacaca on his way to Oruro. I decided to leave.

It was my nineteenth birthday, my first away from home. As I packed, I felt eager and hopeful: definitely, I wouldn't delay, as soon as I was in Oruro I would find transport to La Paz. I opened the latchless wooden door. Frosty air drifted in, while on to the floor of packed earth a hot rhombus of sunlight fell. I felt like a child packing for a summer holiday. I was on my way to a real city now.

From Oruro I continued northwards by rail—but not by train. I travelled in a sky-blue bus fitted with special axles enabling it to use the railway line. This was a 'Pullman Express', and it served the capital of Bolivia.

6

LA PAZ

A ROW of jagged white teeth appeared over the horizon, and rose slowly as the 'Pullman Express' rattled nearer to it: the Cordillera Real, the section of the Eastern Cordillera that overlooks La Paz. As the snowy peaks grew taller, signs of humanity began to show like litter on the land. A road swung close to our rails and for the first time since Argentina it was a tarmac road. Old empty mud houses without roofs sailed by. Adobe walls began to string the building together. We passed a yard containing some llamas, with a woman seated just outside. Now we were in a village, properly; except that it was evidently not a village but the edge of a city: another adobe yard was filled with junk, scrap iron, which an Altiplano village would never possess. I noticed this because there was a huge bronze horseman at least fifteen feet tall riding high above the fence, among the old tanks, tubs and beds. He was holding his sword up. He might have been the last President of Bolivia, discreetly removed to the edge of the city after the last coup, hoping with good reason to ride again soon in the central plaza. Few presidents remain in office for long. Six months is usually considered an adequate term, and time for another coup d'état. So for a president to serve for any length of time takes at least twice as long as elsewhere. The quickest way is for two men to swap, like a good wicket partnership in cricket.

Soon there were streets alongside the railway line, and plenty of people, and cars. I hadn't seen modern cars like these for months. Taxis too, painted yellow and black. Some boys shouted up at the train-bus as it rocked by. And then I saw La Paz. Not this ugly oversized village on the flat plain, but the real city.

It lay below. As we came closer to its edge the whole bowl of La Paz opened beneath, a huge cauldron sunk into the Altiplano, a crater. On its far side a great curving wall of dwellings rose up and up until the wall was too steep for them and became a brown row of hills. Beyond these rose a huge snowy mass, Mount Illimani. I saw it all: the mass of earthen homes crowding the sides of the bowl as high as they could; churches like white rocks here and there; and down in the bottom a little cluster of tall thin buildings, the diminutive skyscrapers of which Paceños are proud.

We came over the edge of the crater and began a slow descent to its floor, zigzagging back and forth first through eucalyptus groves, then along the middle of streets of adobe houses, and finally among the concrete buildings of downtown La Paz.

Then out of the station on my feet into a busy street, a wide dusty avenue with yellow grass dying in a central reserve. Buses and cars thundered by, horns blaring. Every bus had a tiny carpet spread right along the ledge at the bottom of the windscreen, and tiny curtains with tassels hanging at the top of the windscreen. The pavements were flowing with citizens dressed in white shirts, ties and dark suits; the buildings above them were of grey concrete stuck here and there with plain shop and office signs; and I was disappointed. Now that I was here, this was just another western city, a dull-looking one at that, despite its situation. Instinctively I headed for the Indian quarter, the only part of La Paz that seems to belong on the Altiplano.

It is up on one wall of the bowl. As I climbed, the asphalt of the streets gave way to cobbling; litter and grime and rotting vegetable matter gathered on the pavements; the streets narrowed; more people filled them, replacing the cars; and soon I was picking my way among Indian women seated on the ground to sell their goods. The air was sweet with the smell of ripe and rotting fruit—oranges and bananas from the jungle beyond the Cordillera Real, which the women sold—and filled with the noises of Cholos buying and selling.

It was up here that I found a hotel; a painted sign bolted on to the railings of a slim first-floor balcony directed me down a covered alleyway, into the heart of a block. I came out in a concrete courtyard. Under a sloping corrugated iron roof on the far side stood a small wooden table. At the table sat an Indian boy in a white shirt and blue nylon slacks, a boy of twelve or thirteen. He was poring over a book.

He flipped back his mop of hair and smiled up at me. 'Buenas tardes señor,' he sang.

'Buenas. Do you have any rooms?'

'Sí, sí.' He opened a drawer in the table, drew out a small hard-covered exercise book, set the book on the table, tried to slap the drawer shut with an imperious gesture of his left hand, but it stuck half way; then he grinned at me. 'Espera,' he cried, and ran off through a door behind.

A moment later he reappeared with his mother in tow. She was a middle-aged Indian woman, plump but wrinkled as yet only around her mouth, which she held open in more of a grin than a sneer; she wore typical dress, a couple of wide skirts, one on top of the other, one red, one yellow, and a brilliant blue woollen cardigan. She wore no hat, however, so the parting between the two bodies of her hair, each pulled tight on her scalp by the plaits that hung on either side of her head, was plainly visible, as if a white line had been painted there.

'How many days are you staying?' She smiled.

'About three,' I answered.

'Don't you want to meet some other gringos?' she asked.

The question took me by surprise, firstly because of the friendly concern for me that it showed, secondly because so far I had met no other European travellers in Bolivia and doubted that there were any. I replied, 'Sí.'

'Bueno.' Then she looked at me as if worried and said, 'Don't you have a family at home?'

'Sí.'

'And are they coming here?'

'No.'

'And when are you going back home?'

'In two or three months' time.'

'And where are you from?'

'England.'

'Ay. Inglaterra. How can you be so far away for so long?'

The only answer I could think of was, 'No problem.'

She fixed me with her shining black eyes, grinning, and then shook her head. 'Buen, show him room seven,' she told her son, giving him a key from a pocket in her skirt.

He scampered up a staircase, and waited for me on a long balcony that overlooked the courtyard. There were three rooms off this gallery, and the door of the middle one was open. The boy gave me the key and said, 'There's the room,' waving towards the open door. With that he was gone.

I admired the view for a moment: over the corrugated iron roof on the far side of the courtyard I could see much of La Paz, a crater filled with humanity, and looming over all the bustle of the city the white peaks of Mount Illimani hovered, emblems of stillness above. I was flushed with excitement for an instant: it was an exotic city that lay before me: I would eat well, drink well, buy newspapers, meet people, collect my mail, and yet still be surrounded by Altiplano people. Suddenly the previous months of isolation were behind me. I had crossed the emptiest part of the Altiplano. I was within easy reach, once more, of my own life. I could even telephone home. And it was already clear that urban Indians were quite unlike the remote mountain peoples. My landlady already seemed a friend.

Heaving my bag off my shoulders I swung it through the open doorway, its weight pulling me in after.

'Hola.' A voice startled me.

I looked. There were four beds in the windowless room, and on one of them a brown-bearded young white man in khaki trousers reading a paperback.

'Helloo,' came another voice from the other side of the room: a balding, bearded, blond man, long and thin, in a sleeveless sweater and jeans. A heavy pair of boots stood on the floor by his bed.

The woman hadn't given me a room to myself. I was about to go back down and complain indignantly, when the fair man said in English: 'I'm Geoff, by the way.' He had a thick Glaswegian accent.

'Unt I am Rudolf,' said the other in an extraordinary German accent.

It was already too late. I couldn't leave without seeming rude now. I introduced myself and sat down on a free bed.

It was then that I noticed how unusual a sleeping-bag Rudolf was lying in: both his arms and legs were in the open air, protruding from holes. I commented on this.

He scowled at me over the book. 'Ya, ze Austrian army gave me zis unt I make some changes,' he said in his high, piercing voice. He climbed out to show me: 'Look, I cut here across the centre so I can put my legs outside. And I cut here and here so my arms can be outside too. The problem is it's not warm anymore, realmente. And I didn't know South America is so cold.' He pulled his heavy eyebrows into a severe frown.

Rudolf was from northern Austria. He was in his late twenties and worked as a computer programmer. One morning as he was walking to work he passed a travel agent's window on

106

which a very cheap flight to Lima was advertised. In his lunch
break he went and bought the ticket, because it was so cheap,
and three days later, without a word to his mother or friends,
he packed up what he still had of his national service kit and
flew to Peru. From Lima he had travelled south through the
coastal desert into Chile, and then out to the Isla de Chiloe, an
island off Chile, where he had camped for a fortnight, amus-
ing himself by making a set of chesspieces out of shell and
wood. A rag torn from an old check tablecloth served as the
board. He kept his chess set in a long black sock that hung
from his belt and swung as he walked.

'Stupidamente,' Rudolf explained, 'I learned nothing about
South America before I came. When I arrived in Lima there
were clouds every day. There is much cloud and rain in Austria, I didn't need any more. So I looked in my book for the
driest place in South America. It said the driest place is Arica
and Arica is not so far from Lima. Good, I thought, I am lucky.
So I go to Arica. Look: Arica is a desert town. My book told me
it hasn't rained in Arica in the twentieth century. The day I
arrived in Arica it rained all day and all night. The people were
dancing in the street all night. And I couldn't find a hotel so
I lay underneath a lorry in this sleeping-bag. I was so cold and
wet I wished I had never cut here and here and here. And in
the middle of the night I woke up and the lorry was driving
away. I thought I was going to die. But there was nothing I
could do. The lorry was already moving. So I just lay on my
back and waited to die. But the lorry went away without
touching me. Then I got realmente wet.'

Rudolf, whose surname was Sauer, scowled almost continually, even when he was laughing.

Geoff was a merchant seaman in his thirties, a single man,
who spent his leaves hiking in mountains. He had hiked in
many parts of the Old World; this was his first time in South
America. He was a slender and strong man, his tendons and
muscles all visible in relief on his arms and neck. He traveled
with only a small canvas rucksack of an old design, beltless,
so all the weight was taken by the shoulders. His eyes were

blue and bright, his face gaunt, his short gingery beard uneven in density: a furry channel descended from his bottom
lip to his chin, flanked by bare spaces that gave into the
scrubby covering on his lower cheeks. Shallow, long dimples
broke open when he smiled.

He had just returned to La Paz from three weeks' skirting
the snowline in the Cordillera Real, and would be off again in
a day or two into the high mountains. Geoff hiked in places so
remote that he seldom met any other human beings.

We talked through the afternoon and became friends. I
rhapsodized about the Altiplano with excessive eagerness;
this was the first chance I had had to tell anyone in person
about what I had seen, and these two solitary travellers
proved a willing audience. Neither of them had explored
the Altiplano, and both determined to do so. I didn't yet realize
it, but on reaching La Paz I had reached the southern end of
the Gringo Trail, the trail of cities and sites worn by the ex-
changing of travellers' tips and then paved by budget guide-
books. I had just contributed to the making of a new southern
extension.

Standing on the balcony looking out across the hotel yard, I
could see the whole deep bowl of La Paz gathering darkness,
drawing it down from high up in the sky. The sandy red walls
which loomed above became blue and closed in from all
around. From across on the far side of the bowl the thick
covering of houses, so thick that for once the rock they stood
on was unseen, sent out a thousand points of light. Through
the endless noise of the city came the sight of Illimani. Its
lonely peaks were faintly luminous. It is a strange mountain,
a great mass of ice. It hovered in the dark twilight like some
forgotten guardian of the city, a rejected mother. Illimani
almost seemed to have a soul, the way it overlooked the spread
of stars pricking the city beneath.

In fact the Aymaras believe Illimani does have a soul. Illimani is one of the mountains of the Cordillera Real, or Royal
Ridge. On the far side of it are deep valleys clad in jungle

lower down and feeding Amazonia with their endless torrents and waterfalls. Some Aymaras live among the valleys. They hold whatever snow-covered peaks they can see to be potent spirits. The bigger the mountain the more powerful it is, though its size in the eye is what matters: a small mountain very near by may be more powerful than a huge mountain far away. What sort of power do they have? Power to send storms, disease, drought, frost, snow. And to yield up new souls from among the souls who dwell within their flanks. And to feed mankind. On the mountain of Kaata to the northwest of Illimani there are three Aymara villages all at different altitudes. Each village has a distinct ecology and each must feed the mountain with its own produce in an annual series of rituals. Without this balanced diet Kaata would cease to yield crops; disease would be rife; hail would fall endlessly; no more babies would be born. Altogether, the inhabitants live at the mercy of their guardian.

No Aymaras live on Illimani. But all who see her acknowledge her importance as the seat of the souls of La Paz. Moreover, a scholar of the last century proved that the Aymaras originated at the foot of Illimani. He also discovered that the Aymaras were the original stock of all mankind. Thus it is at the foot of Illimani that the Garden of Eden is to be found.

As it grew dark Illimani glowed ever more faintly, until night hid La Paz's mountain entirely. Its disappearance seemed to unstifle the noise of the city. The shouts of vendors and hagglers in the streets were suddenly louder and came more thickly. Even without seeing it I could hear that La Paz is the largest permanent market on the Altiplano, and therefore the most exciting city. For the market has always been one of the two things that break up the monotony of Andean life. Like the fiesta, the market grants a brief escape from the fields, from the perpetual exchange with Pacha Mama, and brings Indians from separate villages into contact with one another.

The city has swelled enormously in the last two centuries. At first it was a mere staging post between Potosí and Lima.

Even now it is still neither the constitutional capital of Bolivia nor the seat of government, both of which are at Sucre (a town not a tenth of the size of La Paz). But in every other way it is the chief city, and calls itself the highest capital in the world. Today women from all over Bolivia bring their goods to La Paz. They sell out on the street, in small temporary stalls or sitting on the pavement. Only the lowliest market women come into the city for the odd day or two, for Chola women do all they can to stay in La Paz. Their goal is a permanent stall in a covered market. To achieve it they have to do as much business as possible. They have to forge links with other women who bring in their produce from the countryside so that they can buy goods themselves to resell. They need suppliers, in other words. But they also need to be sure of buyers. The way they secure supply and demand is by building up a network of contacts, other women. Some of the great queen-bee market women have contacts in every town of the Altiplano who send them their best produce. But the way a connection is first made is always with a debt: either produce is supplied before it is paid for, or it is paid for in advance. And the women call their contacts *ainis*.

The market women have developed their own private *aini* system to match their husbands'. Of course the women's *ainis* have nothing to do with fiestas. But the women have formed a prestige system very like the men's. The more *ainis* a woman has the more respected she is. There is a hierarchy of market women. The higher up the hierarchy her contacts are, the higher she herself is pulled. There's even a Committee of the Union of Merchants, who are the female equivalents of the syndicate secretaries. And at the very top, the president of the Union, female counterpart to the mayor. And the only way a woman can rise in the world is by forging contacts, by handing out effective loans, by opening relations of mutual aid, by helping others because she knows they will help her, in other words by making *ainis* just as the men do. Reciprocity is the keynote of Andean life.

But whereas the men's prestige system leads them into

spending more and more money, the women's enables them to earn more and more money. While the men throw their money into fiestas the women are busy breadwinning.

The streets are full of lights and confusing surges of people. Everywhere there are women sitting on the pavement selling things, each one with her kerosene lamp, which only makes the city seem darker. There are simple cloth canopies under which people sit on benches eating. Rudolf and I turn down one narrow street made even narrower by the stalls which leave room for only a rivulet of bodies between them, following Geoff to the best and cheapest place to eat. Each stall has a canopy above so that the street almost seems roofed, except that it falls so steeply down the hill that I can see right over the canopies below. Behind the wide counters stand Chola women, only their shoulders and heads visible over the produce spread before them. These stalls sell a huge variety things, from plastic soap dishes to bananas and tights. The women's faces shine more clearly than you ever see them elsewhere, the wrinkles making black shadows especially round the corners of the mouth. Between the stalls along the centre of the street, what space there is is crammed full of people, some trying to buy, most trying to get past the buyers.

In another street there is a triangle of space by a junction. Here on the dusty ground Chola women have set up food stalls: big canvas canopies spread high over tables with plastic tablecloths and simple benches. The women squat beside camping gas stoves with huge black frying pans. They fry meat and chopped potatoes in dark oil. They put the food on tin plates and bring it to the table with a little torn square of paper which carries a tiny heap of salt. The customers eat with aluminium spoons.

But Geoff knows a better place and leads Rudolf and me through a doorway off a lane and up a staircase into a huge high hall like a banqueting hall on the second floor above all the stores in the street. This hall is partitioned by sackcloth screens into many little rooms, each one the cell of a Chola woman, who feeds her customers like the women in the stalls outside. But these women have a Union and a Committee and have done well to get their space in here. They constantly have full tables. There is always a straggle of people in the centre of the hall waiting for a seat. Each customer pays a dollar. The women make hundreds a week.

Geoff headed for a woman who had cooked for him before.

'Hola gringos!' she cried.

She was a young woman, fattened out but not yet wrinkled. All the girls suddenly fatten at puberty. They stay ordinary-looking till the fourth or fifth child. Then they abruptly become old-looking. This woman, still unwrinkled, was evidently set for a brilliant career; she had a stall in here already.

She stood at a stove laden with huge saucepans and wide blackened frying pans which hissed and spat at her. As we arrived she was cutting a slice of steak from a carcass that hung beside her from a meat hook.

'What do you want?' she asked. 'Hay bisteck, hay lomito, hay caldo de gallina, hay chorillana, hay churrasco, hay saltado—what would you like? But you'll have to wait a moment for a seat,' she added, looking at her pan as she laid a raw steak in the noisy oil.

'I'll have a chorillana,' said Geoff.

'What's that?' I asked him.

Guessing my question, the woman piped in: 'It's with onions, tomatoes, bananas, a fried egg, fried potatoes, and rice. *Rico.*'

It sounded ingenious. Soon we had seats and our heaped plates arrived, the mass of cooked fruit and vegetables quite concealing the steak at the bottom of each pile. Rudolf ate fast, hardly chewing, like me. But Geoff, who was sinuous and excessively fit, used his fork and spoon carefully, with restraint. After each mouthful he would run a finger under his moustache, finish chewing, and take a swig of beer. I didn't touch my beer until I had wiped my plate clean with bread, and then I drained it at a draught. It was the best food I had had in months.

112

And there was more to come: the woman gleefully cooked us banana pancakes with jam. 'Ay, you gringos need a lot of food,' she laughed.

When I had washed everything down with a second beer I asked her: 'Are you a Paceña?'

She answered me over her shoulder as she cooked: 'No, no. I come from Guaqui, on Lake Titicaca. But I first came to La Paz as a little girl, with my mother, to sell onions. I loved it so much I made her take me every week. Until she got a fixed stall. Then we started living in La Paz.'

'Do you ever go back to Guaqui?'

'Sí, sí. At least once a month. To see my husband and father and brothers.'

'Don't you miss them?'

'No.' She shrugged her shoulders. 'I love La Paz.'

Two Cholo men were standing by the table in dusty suits holding their hats in front of them. One leaned forwards to ask if we had finished. They both nodded appreciatively as we left.

'Come back tomorrow, gringos,' the woman called after us.

Here in La Paz the women are sitting out in the streets selling and selling. A swollen moon, now on the wane, has risen over the rim of the sunken city. This is one Bolivia, the Cholo Bolivia. Out on the barren waves of the Altiplano is another, the old one from which it grew, where it will be cold now under the moon. For with neither water nor vegetation to absorb the heat of the sun during the day, the hills and flat plains exhale only their own iciness at night. Even in the day the sun only heats directly. Any shade, however small, even of a wall, is cold. It is no wonder that the Incas worshipped the sun. The Aymaras at Tiahuanaco worshipped the sun too, as much as fifteen hundred years earlier. But for a different reason. Like the Chipayas they knew the sun had risen for the first time with a new phase of the world and had killed off nearly all the Urus. It had brought drought then, and was still parching their land: they feared its destructive powers.

Whereas the Incas saw the warmth that the sun gave, the Aymaras saw and still see the land, their divine Pacha Mama, from whom they live, drying up and able to give less and less. The Aymaras also knew that before the sun existed the moon had allowed the fertility of Pacha Mama to flourish.

So when the moon shines, bathing the huts and their straw roofs in its light which grants them not so much another aspect as another phase of existence—the old phase, before the sun—the Altiplano reverts to its pristine condition. So much about the Andes is sun and moon: the sun the new, and the moon the old. The market, once a rare event, is now grown into the determining activity of Indian life: as the Incas took up sun-worship so the Cholos have taken up marketing. It is now the sun that outshines their superstitious beliefs. When the Cholos come to La Paz they turn their backs on Pacha Mama.

7

TIAHUANACO

AFTER the Second World War a number of Austrians emigrated to Bolivia. Some set up mining companies in the jungle valleys, others forestry concerns in Amazonia; they remained an inconspicuous community. But one Viennese opened a coffee shop in downtown La Paz, the Café Wien, which became popular with the European diplomats. Rudolf had been visiting it every afternoon since he arrived in La Paz a week ago, at first because he loved cafés, and then because its owner, who kept several chess sets for the use of his customers, had organized a knockout chess tournament that had been running for the last four days. I went there for lunch with Rudolf the day after I reached La Paz.

We walked down from the Indian quarter, away from the cobbled and crowded streets and on to a wide concrete avenue that led to La Paz's only roundabout, Plaza Tiahuanaco.

On one side of it stood the football stadium, and on the others concrete blocks of flats. As we were walking round it I noticed five massive stone faces peering over the metal barrier surrounding the central island. They were monoliths from Tiahuanaco, the ancient centre of the great Aymara Empire.

Rudolf turned to me and said, 'It was an Austrian who *stupidamente* moved them here. *Probablamente* they would look much better in Tiahuanaco.'

We waited for a break in the flow of yellow and black taxis and buses with their festooned windscreens, this being the busiest point in La Paz's network of streets, then crossed to the centre. There below, marooned on this island in the traffic, stood thirty or forty carved monoliths, all of them staring straight at us with enormous vacant eyes; and five were tall enough to look over the walls of the sunken courtyard, an attempt at a reconstruction of the 'Semi-subterranean Temple' at Tiahuanaco from which they were removed in 1948, that contained them.

They were rectangular blocks, the tallest about twenty-five feet tall, most a few heads higher than a man. They had been carved into anthropomorphic figures, but very crudely, in relief. They had faces and arms and legs, but the legs were suggested merely by grooves down the middle; and the arms were pressed tightly into the chests, retaining the shape of the blocks. Some held long unidentified objects in their hands. They had no fingers. But strangest were their faces: wide staring eyes, smooth, high Indian cheeks, open mouths. They seemed to stare with inane astonishment at the modern city in which they found themselves.

Who carved them? Aymaras, when they held their great empire and made Tiahuanaco its religious and political centre. Tiahuanaco is out on the bleak Altiplano, between La Paz and Lake Titicaca. The Spaniards reached Bolivia at least five hundred years after the collapse of the Aymara Empire. When they pressed south from Lake Titicaca and came upon Tiahuanaco, already in ruins, none of the locals could tell them anything about the structures' origins. Nor could the

Incas. In fact, the Incas revealed that even the place's real name was lost. It was they who had called it Tiahuanaco. When the Inca emperor Tupac Yupanqui was campaigning against the Aymara kingdom of Colla he camped by the ruins for a while. One day a messenger arrived from Cuzco who had made the journey so quickly that the Inca told him he was as swift as a guanaco, the fastest of the Andean cameloids. Sit and rest, guanaco, the Inca said to him: 'Tiay, guanaco,' in Quechua, the language of the Incas. And this became the place's name.

Neither the Incas nor the locals could tell the Spanish conquistadors who had built Tiahuanaco. They didn't even know if human beings had built it: some said that the god Viracocha had turned a race of proto-humans into stone, and they were the monoliths that stood in the Semi-subterranean Temple; others said a race of giants had been petrified at Tiahuanaco because they had led sinful lives; still others that the monoliths came to life at night under the moon and guarded untold treasure buried beneath the temples. This last rumour interested the Spaniards most.

In the two decades following the conquest of the Incas *encomiendas* were granted to the conquistadors by their leaders. These were vast estates on which the *encomendero* was responsible for converting the natives to Christianity and from which he received a tribute sufficient to allow him a life of great luxury.

The first encomendero of the encomienda within which Tiahuanaco fell was Captain Juan de Vargas. While he was away in Spain he was visited one night in his sleep by a spirit who said to him: 'You are lord of the richest town in the world.' And the ghost pointed on a map to where his wealth lay: in the ruins of Tiahuanaco.

As soon as the captain was back in Upper Peru he went to his encomienda and began excavations. First he found a giant skeleton; then many gold beads; finally a head of gold carved like the figures in the monoliths above ground. He went to bed overjoyed, full of expectations of more and greater treasures. But that very night he died in his bed. The excavations were stopped, in alarm, and never resumed.

Rudolf was standing with one foot on the metal barrier, an elbow on the raised knee, stroking his thin brown beard and frowning at the monoliths. 'Since I arrived in La Paz I have been wanting to go to Tiahuanaco,' he cried over the noise of the circling vehicles. 'I would like to see where these were realmente meant to stand. Maybe if I lose my match today we could go there tomorrow.'

'We must,' I said. I was already determined to know more about Tiahuanaco.

'Good. But now I am hungry,'

The Café Wien was further along the avenue, on the ground floor of a nondescript edifice of the 1950s. To my surprise, it had been fitted more or less like any other small urban Bolivian restaurant: a short wooden counter with glass-fronted shelves beneath; a few dark polished wooden tables; and several cupboards with glass doors along one wall. In these were trays of plain pastries, a few neatly iced cakes, and one cupboard was full of the special La Paz empanadas. These were like Cornish pasties in shape, and contained a meat and vegetable stew cooked in a sweet sauce, dark brown and thin. They were exceptionally good.

It was just past noon, and any other establishment would have sold out of empanadas by now, for white Paceños eat them for breakfast. But Herr Muller of the Café Wien made a point of getting his in late, so the customers could have them as a light lunch.

He stood behind the counter in a white apron. He had two plumes of silver hair falling from either side of his shining pate, and a bushy silver moustache. He greeted Rudolf with a nod. 'Coffee and empanada?' he asked.

'For two.'

It wasn't yet the lunch hour, and only one table was occupied. We sat and ate our delicious pasties, and ordered two more. We followed them with strong coffee.

When Herr Muller brought the coffee, Rudolf asked him if

he knew why the Tiahuanaco monoliths had been moved from Tiahuanaco.

'It was an engineer called Posnansky who did it,' he said in Spanish, for my benefit. 'When he saw Tiahuanaco he decided to become an archaeologist. And he was the first man to study the place properly. He devoted himself to it for many years. He wanted people to see the ruins, but nobody ever visited them. So he decided to try to persuade the government to move the statues into the city. And of course they were happy to do it: they thought more people would come to La Paz then. As a matter of fact, it made no difference. No difference at all. Still nobody looks at them. Who stops his car on a roundabout?'

'But did Posnansky find out much about the history of Tiahuanaco?' I asked.

Herr Muller smiled and looked over our heads out of the window. 'He showed me some things he wrote, you know. All he ever learned, really, was just how little has ever been known about Tiahuanaco.'

As the café filled with its lunchtime clientele I left Rudolf to play his match, and spent the next four hours trying to establish the place and time of the departure of the bus to Tiahuanaco. Finally, after walking up and down the hills of La Paz several times, I came across the right company's office: a green corrugated iron kiosk the size of a telephone box. A drunken young mestizo in a tracksuit top inside told me through a hatch that it was impossible.

'Impossible to go to Tiahuanaco?'

'Sí. There are no buses to Tiahuanaco.'

'None at all?'

'None.'

'Never? Not tomorrow?'

'Ah. Sí, tomorrow there is a bus that passes Tiahuanaco.'

'But I want to go tomorrow. Or maybe the next day.'

'Well, the bus leaves in the morning, every day.'

'What time?'

'In the morning.'

'What time is that?'

He rocked his head. 'Around seven. Depends how much we drink tonight.' He roared with laughter and raised an unlabelled bottle to his mouth.

When I returned to the hotel room Rudolf was already there, defeated.

'So we will go tomorrow,' he frowned at me.

We were up at six. I set up my kerosene stove on the floor of the hotel room, and made porridge. Rudolf sat on the edge of his bed with a bowl of it between his feet, into which he mashed two little red bananas, the kind that have the strongest flavour. These were his favourite bananas.

Geoff packed up his rucksack, slipped the straps over his shoulders, shook our hands, and strode out of the room to find a truck to take him to the foot of the Cordillera Real for ten days' hiking.

At six thirty in the morning, when it was light but the sun hadn't yet appeared over the rim of the city's crater, the streets of the Indian quarter were quiet. There were no women sitting along their walls. Instead, they laboured up and down the steep thoroughfares with great loads of produce stuffed into bulging sacks made of a shiny white material. A few sweet and cigarette vendors had already set up their trays on street corners. Some restaurants were open for coffee—simple, small restaurants with formica tables and grimy walls. The city was cool.

As we climbed out of the sleeping bowl of La Paz, the bus shaking round bend after bend, the clouds that had spent the night at the foot of Illimani had already stirred themselves into a milky wakefulness and would soon rise to disperse in the thin sky. Then we ground across the Altiplano for an hour. Most passengers were going to Desaguadero, a town on the Peruvian frontier and at the mouth of the river of the same name. We were the only people to get off at Tiahuanaco. This wasn't surprising. Tiahuanaco itself is no more than a hand-

ful of houses dropped on to the plain, which stretches flat and
uninterrupted to the far-off Cordillera Real. The village is as
deathly as if it were deserted, a mere carcass of a human
habitation. And there is no sign of the ruins which have made
it famous.

The bus rattled away, drawing after it a few vapours of
dust. Then three young boys shuffled up to us and opened
their palms to reveal little fake carvings. They were made of
pieces of limestone the size of matchboxes, and depicted the
sun god from the lintel stone of the Tiahuanaco Gate of the
Sun.

Every few seconds one of the boys would say, 'Comprame,
comprame,' buy it from me. They were desperate urchins,
dressed in tattered and smeared sweaters, with great bushes
of matted hair sprouting from their heads. They stared at us
vacantly, mouths open, punctuating the quiet with their little
pleas, which came out of their lips almost mechanically as if
they were unaware of speaking, their expressions unchanging.

Rudolf took one of the little stones from an open palm.
'Cuánto?'

'Cien pesos,' the boy said.

'Cien pesos?' Rudolf shrugged his shoulders, giving it back.

'Cincuenta, cincuenta,' all three of them chorused.

He looked at it again, said sí, and pulled the money out of
his pocket. 'For all three of you,' he warned them.

'Sí, sí,' they said, with the earnestness of lying schoolboys.

The sun was well up by now. The air was quite still. We
pulled off our sweaters and rolled up our sleeves while we
walked. The only sound above our footsteps was the clinking
of Rudolf's chess set as it swung from side to side with every
step he took. The ruins of Tiahuanaco lay a mile ahead down
the dusty road.

They were recognizable at first only by the wire-netting
fence which enclosed the site. Behind it there were various
mounds and ditches partially covered by coarse shrubs and
straw, and a few blocks of stone lying here and there, hot by

now under the sun. It looked more like some discontinued construction site than the former centre of an empire.

A wooden hut stood by the padlocked gate. Its hatch was closed. We were too early. I hooked my fingers on to the netting and stared through a wire diamond at the unsettled ground within. The site reeked of neglect. It looked as though excavations had been started and abandoned early on. One could not feel at ease here: no shade, scant and parched vegetation, nobody around. There was an oppressive lethargy in the air, such as people would take siestas to escape.

Rudolf sat back against the hut and unwound his dangling black sock from his belt. In his high, emphatic voice he asked, 'Shall we play chess? In South America there is always time for a game.'

He spread out his cloth board on the ground and began setting out the shell and wood pieces. Someone was approaching on a bicycle, riding along the road from the village. It was a Cholo man in a black suit and hat, who called, 'Buenos días, señores,' as he dismounted and leaned his bicycle against the hut.

'Maybe another time.' Rudolf wrapped up his chess set and stuffed it back like a ball into the toe of his sock.

'Dos, no más?' asked the man. He had silver stubble on his chin.

'Sí.'

He unlocked his hut and opened up the hatch to sell us two raffle tickets, then came out into the sun again to unlock the gate. His hat brim was bent low over his forehead; his double-breasted jacket was buttoned up; he could have passed for a gangster's henchman. Standing up straight once he had opened the padlock, he said, 'Bueno, señores, pase, pase,' and as he ushered us through the gate he took back the tickets he had just sold us, nodding to each of us in turn and muttering, 'Pues, pues,' in a whisper. We waited a moment, not sure if he was going to act as a guide; but he waved us on, pulled the gate to and withdrew into his hut.

Tiahuanaco could hardly be less impressive, at first sight.

There is a hillock not more than twenty feet high: the 'stepped pyramid'. There is a raised platform of paving the size of a tennis court: the Kalasasaya. In the far corner of this stands a doorway: two upright stones and a lintel, the renowned Gate of the Sun. Placed as it is in a corner with rubble and broken blocks littered all around, it seems to have been re-erected without much reverence, as if the restorers had got bored in the middle of their task. Nor is it more than ten or twelve feet tall. And the third major structure of the complex is the Semi-subterranean Temple, another paved tennis court sunk about a yard deep into the ground. The famous monoliths used to stand in here. This sorry place is Tiahuanaco, the ceremonial centre of the great Aymara Empire, the monument of the Aymara's greatest age; and the object of awe and speculation and wonder ever since the Spaniards first saw it.

Archaeologists still do not know exactly who built Tiahuanaco, nor when; their guesses at dates differ by as much as a millennium. They have agreed to call its builders Aymaras, since they may have spoken Aymara; but the only evidence for this is the modern distribution of the language and the absence of any other population in the area. When you think of those Aymaras out on the Altiplano near Sacaca, simple peasants living in villages of scattered adobe huts, it is hard to believe it was their ancestors, who also lived in haphazard mud homes, that built these structures. However uninspiring the ruins are now, those two courts are at least rectangular and well-made. The 'pyramid' also would have had straight sides and clean angles on its long, wide steps. Why did those peasants in their rough, crude houses decide to build a grand ceremonial centre with such rectilinear edifices? How could they even conceive of such things? And, moreover, when the Spaniards first came to Tiahuanaco the plain was almost deserted. So they found these ruins, which bespoke some degree of civilization, in the middle of a semi-desert. What were they doing here? Their bewilderment grew when the only natives they found nearby told them that the ruins had been made by the creator of the world and that the many statues which then stood on the site were in fact men turned to stone by this god because they had misbehaved.

The only thing that is clear is that some kind of elite, probably a religious one, must have existed at the time of Tiahuanaco's construction to organize the building work.

As we were coming down from the summit of the mound that used to be the stepped pyramid, which we had climbed to gain a view of the whole desolate site, the guard in his black suit suddenly appeared over a bank nearby. He waved a long arm at us, beckoning.

We followed. 'This you must see,' he said quietly, leading us down into the Semi-subterranean Temple, stepping erectly and briskly down a flight of five steps into the paved court, 'Mira, señores,' he urged us; and then left.

Once you enter the Semi-subterranean Temple you begin to understand why Tiahuanaco has fascinated people. Ten-oned into the walls of the temple are hundreds of small stone heads. They are human heads: they have eyes, nose and mouth; but none of the features are realistic. They stare with the most cold and empty stare imaginable. When you stand in the middle of the temple you are surrounded by heads jutting out from the walls, craning their necks to stare at you, fixedly and penetratingly. Yet the strangest thing is that they aren't really looking at you. Look one of them full in the face—and it isn't looking at you, even though its eyes stare at you. It is looking through you, and through the opposite wall, and through the ground behind the wall; it is looking through everything, through the material world. And it is not just one head doing this, but hundreds of them. Surrounded by them, all looking clean past your world, all seeing something which you cannot see, as if there were some phantom hovering where you stand, invisible to you but perceptible to them, you feel unnerved. Perhaps you even feel something of the Aymaras' superstitious fear.

For these stone heads are embodiments of Aymara spirits: a league of spirits incarnated in stone. So they see only their own spiritual world, the world in which the Aymaras believe though they never see it themselves. This must have been a terrifying place for Aymaras.

The carved monoliths that Posnansky the Austrian took to La Paz used to stand here, filling the court. He left three behind, the most weatherbeaten ones. They have almost been smoothed into the blank blocks they originally were. But you can still make out the faces of these petrified beings, and they have the same metaphysical stare as the heads in the wall. They are very thin, each one not more than a foot square at the base. They make a gaunt trio, abandoned by their worshippers and their companions. Their faces, worn by the wind and rain, show how ephemeral is even the most solid product and record of a civilization: even monumental art vanishes.

The guard was back, beckoning us again from up above, outside the sunken courtyard. 'Venga, señores,' he called.

He led us up on to the Kalasasaya, the raised court, and over to the Gate of the Sun that stood in a far corner. 'Mira, señores'; and he hopped down from the platform and again disappeared, to leave the ruins, as ever, to speak for themselves.

The great portal stands massive and inconsequential, re-erected in a corner of the court, leading nowhere. Its two upright supporting stones are very neatly cut and shaped; but it is the lintel stone, carved in relief on one face, that has won renown. In the centre of the relief is a deity, a squat figure holding a condor-headed sceptre in either hand and with rays radiating from his head. Because of these, this deity has for centuries been interpreted as the sun god. But cautious modern archaeologists refer to him as the Doorway Deity. Whether or not he is the sun, he is weeping: and his tears roll down his cheeks in the form of jaguars. On either side are rows of bird-headed men who come running towards him. These have been identified as demons and as messengers. One thing is clear, they are his subjects: he is twenty times their size.

The Gate of the Sun has been seen for a long time as the earliest evidence of sun-worship in the Andes, as a precursor to the Incas' religion. But even if the deity is not the sun, the symmetry, geometric precision and central focus of the design still suggest that whoever carved it had noticed some sort of order in the world, and did not believe that the world was governed by a rabble of unruly spirits. It seems the product of a higher religion than the Aymaras' superstition. Like the temples of Tiahuanaco, the Gate of the Sun speaks of civilization, a large, ordered society, not a littering of mud villages. And again, it has mystified Europeans because of the lack of any apparent remnants of the population that built it.

There is one clue to the riddle of Tiahuanaco: its old Aymara name. The Aymaras called it Paypicala: Stone in the Middle.

In some Aymara myths when the creator of the world, Viracocha, arose from the waters of Lake Titicaca to create humankind, he went to Paypicala and made a troop of stone beings. Then, turning to each of the cardinal points, he bade men come forth out of the ground. Mankind emerged in bands. Viracocha designated one of his statues to be a symbol for each band, a totem for that lineage. Thus each branch of mankind had its statue at Paypicala, its own Stone in the Middle. And all the Aymaras scattered over the plain could turn towards Paypicala and acknowledge it as the one real centre of humanity.

Yet at the same time the many different places, the caves, the mountaintops, the rocky outcrops, the springs, the hillocks, where the separate bands of humankind had emerged from the earth, these too could be revered as the point of origin of the local tribe. So the Aymaras did live in their scattered villages and they did worship their diverse spirits, yet nevertheless they had one all-embracing centre: Stone in the Middle. Just as each Aymara baby has a little flint knife buried in the floor of the house where it was born, so the whole of humanity, as far as the Aymaras were concerned, had its stones in the centre of the world, at the place where all men were conceived: the monoliths, the massive stone stakes, of Tiahuanaco. Which have now been moved.

Recent archaeology has proved that there never was a large population living near Tiahuanaco. Tiahuanaco was never a city, nor even near a city. It was always an isolated ceremonial centre. The population it served, like the Aymaras of today, lived in scattered villages. They would have congregated for the construction of the site, and for worship in it; which says much for their beliefs. For the sake of religion, they surpassed themselves by as much as Tiahuanaco does their villages.

'Qué te parece?' the guard asked me as we walked out of the wire gateway. What did you think? He was holding the gate open for us.

'Interesante.'

'Interesante, no?' He was looking up at me, standing very erect and stiff, and smiling expectantly. For a moment I thought he was waiting for a tip. Then he said: 'Would you like to see something?'

He went into his hut and came out carrying a block of stone the size of four or five bricks. Despite the weight he stepped briskly over to a fence post against which he set down his burden, and stood next to it with his arms folded. 'Mira, pues,' he said. Look, then.

What had at first seemed the roughness of the stone resolved itself into a carving in relief of a square head with circular eyes and a slim rectangular mouth, similar to the face of the sun god on the Gate of the Sun. With the sun falling full on it, the relief was almost concealed by the absence of shadows.

'Qué te parece?' asked the guard. Was it his? Had he found it? Did he think we were archaeologists? Or antique dealers? Or was he simply proud of his ancestors' art, and of his post as keeper of it? His straight back and faintly smirking face seemed to evince pride.

'Bonito,' I said politely.

'Has encontrado o has hecho?' came Rudolf's piercing voice. Did you find it or make it?

'Sí, sí,' said the guard. 'I found it myself. Just on the other side of the Kalasasaya.' He nodded to confirm this; and then said, 'Bueno, pues,' abruptly, picked up his stone and took it back to its place in his hut. He was offended. He shut the door after him. He must have sat on a stool, for his face appeared dimly in the chest-high hatch; and it remained still, staring out across the empty plain.

We walked back to the village: two rows of houses facing one another across a dusty street, whose adobe had faded to yellow. Every door was closed.

We had two of the hottest hours to wait until the same bus that had brought us passed on its way back to La Paz. Rudolf pulled off his sock once more and said, 'And now we must play.' We slumped against a wall and set up the cloth board on the ground between us. As we made our first moves the same three urchins appeared again from behind a house. They approached us silently, but when they recognized us they stopped where they were, and stood watching in the middle of the road. I looked at them while Rudolf was scowling at the board with his forehead resting on a fist, and their staring, passive eyes struck me as familiar. These boys had the same tireless, vacant expression as the Tiahuanaco monoliths.

The bus arrived an hour late; however, in Bolivia *dos de la tarde* means nothing more exact than soon or quite soon after lunch, so effectively the bus was not late. But in that last hour my concentration failed. I was bored, and Rudolf won each game more quickly. The last one was over in minutes.

Finally the bus wound into La Paz. Then we were stuck in a traffic queue that brought us slowly closer to Plaza Tiahuanaco. As we drove round it I had a last look at the exiled monoliths: they looked more out of place than ever, like a battalion captive behind enemy lines; idols impounded by the invaders, idols whose worshippers remained beyond the intruders' reach.

I got off the bus in the bottom of the city and was just in time to catch the British Consulate for my mail. There were three letters for me, and I read them avidly one after the other, and then reread them, as I made my way slowly up towards the hotel. When I reached the hotel room I lay on my bed to read them over again. Still I had not exhausted the excitement that these three little envoys from home had to offer. They contained no special news; they were all from my family; yet their presence here in La Paz, when a few weeks ago they had actually been in my very home, was exhilarating. I insisted on Rudolf's reading them too, even though they could have been of little interest to him. He acquiesced; and as he finished each one I read it again. They made my journey seem valuable in a way I was normally unaware of: they reminded me that I had a home I would return to, and that when I did I would be a person who had crossed the Altiplano of the Andes. They quite dispelled thought of Tiahuanaco.

The following morning Rudolf and I parted. He was going to head south, and I was on my way to Peru now. We exchanged addresses, and he gave me five little crimson bananas for the journey. We were sorry to leave one another, and did not draw out our farewell.

As I came down the stairs the hotel woman was sweeping the courtyard. I paid her.

'And where are you going now?' she asked, resting her chin on the end of the broomstick and grinning.

'To Peru.'

'Ay, gringuito, you should go back to your family.'

'Sí, sí, señora. I will soon.'

'Bueno,' she said, and laughed briefly. 'Take care in Peru. The Peruanos are not like us.'

I boarded a truck full of Cholos bound for Lake Titicaca. We wound up the chain of hairpin bends that lead out of the bowl of La Paz, and then, once we had reached the open plain, we stopped. All the passengers scrambled out and stood at the side of the road. It was breakfast-time.

A Cholo man had set up a table there, with two camping stoves beside it. On one was a black pan full of oil in which he was deep-frying pancakes. He would roll out dough on the table and then holding the floppy disc on the end of a wire, which every time tore a hole in the pancake, so thin did he roll them, he would lower the misshapen lifeless thing into the oil—which would bubble wildly around the foreign body, and in seconds restore it to a disc, crisp and yellow with a hole in the middle, to be stacked in an enamel bowl on the table.

To go with the pancake the man made a strange drink, *api*. It consisted of two liquids, one dark purple and hot, from a saucepan on the other gas ring, and the other cold and thick and cream-coloured, almost like a gruel, from a jug on the table. This was made of maize; the other from berries. The man would half fill a glass with the thick maize drink, then pour on the steaming purple syrup.

It was a delicious drink, the hot sweetness diluted by the cold nourishing ingredient. Each swig entered the mouth not warm but hot and cold at once, unmixed. With a sugar-sprinkled pancake, it made a good breakfast. The Cholo men and women stood about chewing and slurping noisily, while the sun appeared in a chink in the Cordillera Real and came to us fresh over the frost on the hills.

Three hours later we reached Lake Titicaca, at the Straits of Tiquina. Lake Titicaca is the highest navigable lake in the world, and its altitude makes it extraordinarily blue. Its water looks like paint, a deep, thick blue. Half the earth's atmosphere is beneath it. And all around the blue water stand the sand-coloured hills of the Altiplano.

We climbed out of the truck and watched it board a wooden steel ferry large enough for two lorries. As it moved out on to the blue lake we took our seats around the gunwales of an open wooden fishing boat, and cast off after it. The Chola women sat in silence as we bobbed up and down on the modest waves. Every now and then a peal of raucous laughter from the ferry would reach us over the water.

The crossing took only a few minutes; the Straits of Tiquina are a mile wide. We all clambered back into the waiting truck, and after a few miles winding among the hills, we rolled into Copacabana.

The frontier-post is in this little town, in the hallway of an old colonial house with a parched garden. The border guard sat at a writing table decked with five different stamps, an ink pad and a small Bolivian flag. He was a mestizo, with the smooth cheeks of an Indian and the drooping moustache of a Spaniard. He wore a khaki uniform.

He studied my passport for a long time, elbows on the table, both hands clutching the passport, and then raised his small suspicious eyes, black eyes that looked guilty and made me feel guilty, and said: 'There's no exit stamp.'

'What?'

'You have to have an exit stamp from La Paz.'

'From La Paz?'

'Sí,' and he closed the passport.

When you are on the move from one place to the next, all your anticipation hanging on your destination, it is horrifying to think about turning back, especially when your destination is another country. It had taken five hours to get here from La Paz. Suddenly I was worrying that I would never be able to leave Bolivia. Perhaps this man would even have me thrown in jail for attempting to cross the border unofficially.

Then it occurred to me that there were probably no such things as exit stamps from La Paz.

'Is there no other way?' I asked.

The guard mumbled something, and said, 'Pues.'

'No other way at all?' This was the first time I attempted to offer a bribe. 'What can we do?' I sighed.

But the guard was an old hand, and came straight out with the price. 'Do you have dollars? Five dollars.'

But I was so used to haggling that I instinctively fell into my routine: 'Es mucho, no? Cinco . . . I have very little money.'

We settled it at three dollars. He stamped my passport with three different stamps, and ten minutes later I was in Peru.

8

TITICACA

BOTH Peru and Bolivia straddle the Andes and reach some way into Amazonian forest. Both have a high proportion of Indians in their population. Both were in the Inca Empire. Both are now poor and ill-governed. Yet to a traveller coming from one to the other they seem as different as sunshine and moonlight. Bolivia is a landlocked country, remote and isolated. Peru, with its 1400-mile-long Pacific coast, is open to the world, and easy-going. Coming into Peru from Bolivia is like coming back into a familiar world.

Since the eighteenth century when Bolivia's silver ran out, Peru has grown in wealth and importance and has eclipsed its neighbour. Even before then, it was in Peru that the Incas had their capital, Cuzco. And the Peruvian highlands have always had a wealth of fertile soil. This above all distinguishes the Peruvian and Bolivian high plains. The Peruvian highlands are cut up by tremendous canyons. Some of these are so deep that while the top of a valleyside yields only potatoes, the bottom is in a tropical climate rich in fruit: and between the two grow maize and other cereals. So it is common for a community to live on the Altiplano yet be within a day's walk of bananas and oranges, and a morning's walk of sweet corn. These deep sierra valleys were far more attractive places for Spaniards to settle in than the barren plains of Bolivia. The proportion of pure-blooded Indians in Peru's population is smaller, because there are more Spaniards. Villages untouched by Spanish influence are rare. Those that do exist undoubtedly came under the sway of the Incas: the Inca administration was much more penetrating in all Peru than in Bolivia.

Because of this I no longer felt the urgency to find remote places that I had done in Bolivia. I wasn't going to find isolated, backward Indians leading ancient lives free of all extraneous influences. So I settled, for the time being, into moving along the main roads with a series of lifts in trucks, stopping off in some of the villages along the way.

I was coming in by the southwestern shore of Lake Titicaca. The lake occupies most of the highland frontier between the two countries, which share it equally. It spreads almost from Cordillera to Cordillera, filling the corridor of the Altiplano. It is for this stretch of water alone that the Bolivian Navy, a one-boat navy, exists.

Every village I passed was planted with tall eucalyptus trees shading the streets and houses. The plazas had whitewashed colonial buildings. Around the villages lay green fields of young wheat and corn and onions and down by the lakeside stood great banks of reeds. The Titicaca basin is by far the most fertile region on the Altiplano.

At Chucutio, the ancient capital of the Aymara kingdom of Lupaca, on the western shore of the lake, the weekly market had dissipated within the last hour. A few Chola women still sat on one side of the square, even though the morning shade had moved, selling oranges from sacks. A policeman laughed to a friend and opened a bottle of beer with his teeth. His eyes were already narrowed by drunkenness. All the Aymaras who had come in for the market had left again, for their villages in the hills behind the little town. The Titicaca region is still populated predominantly by Aymaras. It is the northern extent of their distribution.

Like all the Peruvian lakeside towns, Chucuito has a mestizo church: large and whitewashed, with heavy stone carving on its portal. The carvings are of saints. But like the figures of early Christendom, they seem more heathen than Christian: thick, heavy men standing in odd positions. These were among the earliest attempts of Peruvian natives to produce Christian art, although these Indian sculptors were half-European too, which their products seem to show: Christian subject matter, but Andean forms.

The church was locked. Two young men with sharp glints in their eyes appeared from the road and came up swiftly to explain that thieves had stolen everything from the church. That was why it had to be kept locked now.

A little boy with a tiny set of Pan pipes, sampoñas, was wandering round the church. He blew the odd note and then, as boys do with harmonicas, would blast up and down the instrument, running it along from side to side under his lips making a frantic, unnerving sound, quite unlike the usual expansiveness of Pan pipes.

In Puno, the main port of Lake Titicaca, and an ugly modern sprawl, I found out that the most interesting part of the lake is the northern shore. Traditional people still live there. But they are not Aymaras. They are Quechuas.

Nearly all of Peru's Andean Indians are Quechuas, the population that the fallen Inca Empire left to Peru. The Quechuas, once a small people from a valley in southern Peru, became the most widespread Indian group because the Incas adopted the Quechua language and customs as those of the Empire, and enforced them on their subject races. In other words, they turned the peoples of the Andes into Quechuas. Today there are ten million Indians who speak Quechua. Six

hundred years ago, just before the Inca Empire was estab-
lished, there were probably fewer than 30,000.

The Incas sent groups of Quechuas to far corners of their
empire as colonists. They called these groups *mitmas*. They
were also sent to recalcitrant areas, to set an example of loyalty to the Incas, and to act as spies on potential rebels.

The Aymaras of the northern shore of Lake Titicaca were
the Collas. They had long been a powerful kingdom, and it
took two heavy campaigns for the Incas to subdue them. Even
then they remained a volatile subject people. So a Quechua
colony was sent out to settle in their territory, where they
have remained to this day.

Taraco should be a quiet Altiplano town. It stands on the
northern side of the lake, a few miles inland. But it is on the
main road from Puno to the jungle in the east, and its plaza is
always filled with parked lorries. Some are heavy with fruit,
heading back west; some are empty, on their way to Amazonia. The trucks stop here for food.

I arrived in the afternoon. In the centre of the square, under the little trees, were several tables covered with plastic
cloths, in front of them benches, and behind them Chola
women surrounded by huge aluminium saucepans. The
women had plenty of business: people from the parked trucks
standing around the square, both passengers and drivers,
filled the benches to eat bowls of soup and plates of rice with
stew. Around the edge of the square a few women sat selling
fruit and bread.

I approached an orange-seller. She was a young woman
with a smooth brown face. She wore a white hat, the fashion
for Chola women in this area. It was the shape of a floppy
cricket hat, but made of a stiff cloth. Beside her on the ground
lay a hideous mask.

'What's that?' I asked.

'It's a devil,' she said with a grin, holding her head back to
look at me. The sky around my face must have been dazzling
to her. She squinted tightly.

'Un diablo?'

'Yes. There was a fiesta here yesterday. The boys dress up in masks. For the dances.'

'Was it a big fiesta?'

'Sí . . .' she said. 'Un poco.'

So it had been a bit big. I had stumbled on more than my fair share of fiestas in the last few weeks. Still, it was frustrating just to have missed one.

'Where are you from?' the woman asked, throwing up her chin.

'Inglaterra.'

'And your family? Are they here too?'

'No, they're in England.'

'Ah. Very far away.' She folded her hands in the apron she wore over her dress. 'What are you doing here?'

Travelling and writing a book were unsatisfactory answers to this question. You had to have some concrete goal. If you didn't specify one then it was assumed you were concealing it.

'I want to visit ancient people,' I said. This was the standard phrase for traditional Indians.

'What? The Quechuas?' she asked.

'Sí, sí.'

'Why don't you go to Ramis? The Quechuas live there.'

'Where is Ramis?'

'Thirty kilometres from here. Tomorrow morning we all go there in a lorry for a market. They have a market every Saturday. If you want you can come with us.'

'Muchas gracias, señora.'

She laughed, then said: 'Buy my oranges. How many are you having?'

I wandered out from the town towards the river that flowed nearby. I walked along the edges of onion fields. Onions became an important cash crop around Lake Titicaca after the 1952 agrarian reforms. Before then, under the landlords, the peasants had been able to grow almost nothing to sell.

The river, when I reached it, was wide, brown and swift.

This was the Río Ramis, which flows into the lake thirty kilometres downstream, beside the village of the same name. A line of Cholo men stood on the riverbank. Occasionally a man would shout, and another would throw a pebble out into the river. In the middle of the stream a thin totora-reed boat was being punted with immense difficulty by a small man in a drenched suit. He laboured with his pole, apparently trying to lift it out for a new stroke. It must have got stuck. But no: he was moving it. Instead of pulling it up he was scraping it along the bottom. And gradually, foot by foot, he was working his way to the shore. On the little mud beach at the bottom of the bank stood four men who were pulling on ropes that came dripping from deep in the river. Sometimes the man in the boat would shout and they would stop pulling for a moment. When he finally reached the shore I realized what was happening: with his pole he was holding a net down on the riverbed which the men on the shore were tugging in to the side. Was this their way of fishing?

Meanwhile three other reed boats were out in the stream, each with two men standing up. These men had long poles with large two-pronged hooks on the end. They flayed out into the water and pulled their poles in. They were scraping the bottom.

And the men in a line at the top of the riverbank were shouting instructions to the others, indicating places in the river with the pebbles they threw.

A very solemn, middle-aged Cholo walked up and greeted me with a grave nod.

'Buenos días,' I replied.

'Señor, do you have a telescope?' he asked.

'No, I don't.'

He looked at me with what seemed suspicious eyes: perhaps he thought all westerners were always fully equipped with western technology. 'No telescope?' he tried again.

'No.'

He did not seem to believe me.

'But what's going on?' I asked. 'Qué pasa?'

He lowered his head. 'We're looking for someone. That's why we need a telescope.'

'Who?'

'A drowned man.'

'When did he drown?' I asked.

'Yesterday.'

'At the fiesta?'

'Sí.'

Perhaps the man had gone for a swim or fallen out of a boat blind drunk.

Some women sat watching on the bank, their skirts spread wide about them. But this was the men's affair, this drowning. They made a big show of it, not only because they wanted to retrieve the body. Normally the men hover in the dimness outside the centre of Cholo life, marketing. Here was a chance for them to prolong their time in the limelight after the fiesta. So they shouted and ran about and threw stones and dropped their poles in the water—and found nothing.

Early next morning I went by truck to the village of Ramis, with ten of the Taraco market women and their heavy sacks of produce. The truck bounced and jolted along a rough track over the dry suede of the Altiplano, which already shimmered in the distance under a fierce sky. For even here, so near the lake, the Altiplano is parched as anywhere. It is only along the very shore of Titicaca, and in irrigated fields alongside the rivers, that you see green vegetation. From around the deep blue of the lake the land stretches away first in a band of waterlogged green and then as dry and barren as the rest of the plain.

This area on the north side of Lake Titicaca once had an Uru population, long ago, before the Aymaras arrived. On the flat land between the lake and the hills in the middle distance stand endless round adobe huts which turn in at the top to form shallow cones for their roofs. They are like the huts which litter the plain around Chipaya. There, where the plain is flat and still has swamps and shallow lakes, Urus thrived. Here too, where the conditions were once the same.

It was still early, but we were coming to a market. The lorry pulled up on an open space by a small church, and there was not the least sign of anyone else nearby. Had the market been cancelled today? All about stood the strange crop of round huts sprung up on the plain.

The women clambered out and I helped them with their sacks. Immediately they began spreading out sheets and blankets on the ground here and there in front of the church.

Then from the silent huts, the nearest a few hundred yards away, from all around, it seemed, black figures started appearing. They walked towards us slowly, laden with bundles.

The Chola women were ready, each one sitting with a sheet in front of her and her open sacks standing beside her. Some had stacks of oranges too.

The first Quechua women arrived, in dusty black dresses and black shawls over their heads like the shawls the Chipaya women wear. One by one they squatted down in front of the Cholas, on the far side of the sheets. Talking in hushed Quechua, which sounds like whispering, the consonants seeming all sibilants and dentals punctuated now and then by a little guttural sound, they took their bundles from their backs and opened them up. They would put three or four cupped handfuls of grain or beans out on the Cholas' sheets; who, sitting upright, surrounded by their bags, would throw over two oranges, or some dried pimentos, or some sweets, whatever the Quechua wanted. Sometimes the Quechua would say something quietly before she picked up her goods. The Chola, perhaps having retained an orange in her hand, would shake her head and click her tongue. The Quechua would put out half a handful more of grain; and the extra orange would be dropped in front of her. Then she would wrap what she had bought in her bundle, swing it on to her back, and walk on to another Chola.

So it continued, more and more Quechuas arriving, until the whole space in front of the church was filled with the rustling of the black dresses of the women squatting around the blankets and sheets and wandering from Chola to Chola.

It was, as ever, the Cholas' market. They sat unmoved among their produce, merely waiting for Quechuas and chucking over whatever was requested, once the price was right. The Quechuas were the busy bees moving from flower to flower. For them, it was a special event. They whispered, nervous and excited. Some had walked three or four miles, from the furthest scattered huts, to barter what Pacha Mama had yielded.

I walked away from the market, over a small rise of the land, towards Lake Titicaca half a mile away. The ground had been ploughed and patches of corn planted. There was a cluster of adobe homes down by the water. Beyond them a fisherman like a stick in the distance punted his totora boat across the calm surface. I went to the houses, hoping for a glimpse of Quechua domestic life. Pigs and cows were noisily munching corn in the yards. No one was about. On the far side of the hamlet, a little track led down to the lake shore. Here a boy and his mother were pulling up armfuls of reeds and laying them out on the mud to dry. They stopped their work to look at me, said nothing, and went back to it, their sleeves rolled up but their lower garments dangling in the water.

Both the Incas and the Aymaras held Titicaca as the Sacred Lake. From its waters arose the mythical founders of both the great empires, Tiahuanaco and Inca. It is the most fertile place on the Altiplano, as if here Pacha Mama responds at last to the worship and gifts of the Aymaras. The whole shore seems unusually peaceful. The noise of the animals eating, the sound of the quiet human voices, the gathering rise and fall of the land, the deep blue of the water reaching out to the horizon, all make you feel at ease and content.

A man came briskly towards me. He waved a long arm and shouted, 'What are you doing here?' and kept coming.

I was standing just outside the village, at the edge of a little field.

'Yes?' the man said when he reached me. He was flustered. 'Are you an engineer?'

'No.'

'Do you have a permit?' He wore a brown derby tilted back on his head. He had teeth too big for his mouth, like a horse.

'What permit?' I asked.

'A permit to be here. You cannot enter here without a permit.'

I was unaware of having entered anything. Whatever it was I exited, and strolled off to the market again.

By now it was already tailing off. Only a few Quechua women remained. The rest were spread out on the plain, retreating like black monks to their round homes. The Chola women were tying up their sacks and folding away their blankets.

I was back in Taraco by noon. From here I wanted to make my way northwest towards Cuzco by a small dirt track. But after a day and a half of waiting for transport to come along this lonely road, I gave up, and accepted that I would travel to Cuzco by the main road. So I took a lorry from Taraco back to Juliaca, a small bustling town of modern buildings and paved streets. Here I was lucky enough to find a lorry taking a load of mattresses to Cuzco.

It was the most enjoyable journey I ever made. The only passenger, I lay back on the mattresses, which were stacked high enough to allow an unobstructed view of the Altiplano over the sides as sunset and night overcame it. As soon as I felt the cold I pulled on my sleeping-bag. I had all the joys of sleeping out—the stars, the shooting stars which are plentiful so high up, the fresh icy air—and the excitement of rumbling across an empty land at night. The only discomfort was to be woken up by the driver at three in the morning, when I had reached my destination: Combapata, a small village half way to Cuzco.

I was in the plaza. The driver assured me that the house beside me was a hotel and that it would be all right to rouse the keeper. So I hammered at the wooden double doors. The lorry growled out of earshot. There was silence. I knocked again. Finally a Chola woman fully dressed but for her hat opened up. She led me through a shop and upstairs to a long room with six empty beds. I could sleep where I liked. She left me. I resumed my dreams, putting the trials and efforts of tomorrow out of mind: for the next day I would walk high into the Eastern Cordillera, to visit the most remote and undisturbed Quechuas.

9

QUECHUAS

BY THE TIME the Incas began their expansion from Cuzco the Quechuas were a growing people. They had already made satellite settlements outside their own valley, and had not the Incas been growing in strength and territory at the same time it might even have been the Quechuas who forged an empire. They had a few skirmishes with the expanding Incas, but were soon conquered and became such loyal subjects that many were honoured with places among the Inca nobility in Cuzco, while the mass of the increasing Quechua population provided the bulk of the Incas' manpower. It was Quechuas who fought in the Inca campaigns, Quechuas who fed the Incas, at least in the Empire's early years, before it had fully expanded, Quechuas who were sent as colonists to remote rebellious provinces; and Quechua was made the official language of the Empire. If the Incas had not had such a loyal subject people from a valley near their own, they could not have built an empire.

The Inca Pachacuti, or He Who Overturns the Earth, made Quechua the language of the Empire in the middle of the fifteenth century. Today Quechua is still the most widely spoken Indian language. Pachacuti also imposed Quechua customs on his new subjects.

Forty years after the Spaniards reached Peru they founded many towns in which Indians from surrounding villages were resettled. The result was that most Quechuas, brought into permanent contact with the whites, became Cholos. As every town had a marketplace and as marketing increased, even the Quechuas who had escaped resettlement would come into the towns for the weekly market, and so were exposed to Spanish influence. Also, Spaniards settled in many of the remote valleys, setting up small farms and plantations; because of that, Peru now has an extensive road network. The consequence of all these things is that very few villages in Peru remain hidden and isolated; everywhere is accessible.

There are still remote corners where life continues largely unchanged since Inca times. But these places are off the roads and tracks. You have to walk to them. It was to visit one of these areas that I came to Combapata.

Combapata is in the Vilcanota valley. After Lake Titicaca the Altiplano narrows and swings to the northwest, towards Cuzco. The Eastern Cordillera, the eastern wall of the high plateau, turns with it, moving, as you travel north, ever closer to the Western Cordillera until the two finally meet in a turbulent sea of hills in the far north of Peru. A hundred miles beyond Lake Titicaca the narrow Altiplano rises to a bleak pass. On the far side of this is the head of the valley of the Vilcanota river which flows on all the way to Cuzco and beyond. The valley begins as a desolate channel between the hills, along which fierce winds race. But it gradually descends, and becomes the shelter of a string of towns and villages long before reaching Cuzco. This valley was the first conquest that the Incas made, and it was a crucial one: once they had control of it they had a clear route to Lake Titicaca, which was their next area of expansion. It is an important valley for the same reason today: beside the grey water of the river run both the railway and the main road from the lake to Cuzco.

Combapata stands on the eastern riverbank, bushy with the green-silver leaves of eucalyptus trees. In its small plaza the houses are two storeys high and have wooden balconies on the first floor. Their windows have shutters, their fronts are whitewashed. But the rest of the village, apart from the concrete school, is a spread of adobe huts with tin roofs.

I stocked up on bread and oats and sardines, left what I did not need of my belongings with the schoolteacher and set off east up a side valley which would bring me high into the Eastern Cordillera.

In the first two hours of walking I passed three little hamlets which considered themselves suburbs of Combapata. Then my valley closed in and steepened and I began to climb. The brook came tumbling over boulders above and crashed on down to the Vilcanota behind me. There were thorny bushes with little white flowers buzzing with flies and bees. Every now and then a hummingbird would hover into sight from behind a shrub and disappear again. But they were large hummingbirds, which are less colourful than the tiny varieties. I hardly knew them from wrens or small thrushes.

I met one man in the afternoon. He was an Indian in mestizo dress: faded crimson slacks and an old misshapen polo neck sweater. He came round a rock which cut across the path, and almost trotted into me. When Indians walk in the mountains they employ a gait faster than a walk, but not a jog because one foot is always on the ground and because they move very lightly. They manage to keep all their weight travelling forwards while their feet skip along underneath. Whereas I laboured pace by heavy pace, and needed the thick soles of my boots to avoid hammering my feet to shreds.

The man stopped as soon as he saw me. 'Buen tardes,' he sang, his face set in a continuous expression of light-hearted joy, so he did not need to smile.

'Buenas,' I replied. But before I could open a conversation he had shuffled past, to where he apparently believed he was hidden by the large rock, and in one movement pulled down his trousers and sank to a squat to relieve his bowels.

I walked on wondering if the Indians all suffer from permanent diarrhoea.

In the morning I had been at ten thousand feet above sea level. By the evening I was more than six thousand feet higher. I could have climbed more gently, but I was aiming for a high pass and wanted to camp near it so that I would be able to tackle it fit and fresh from sleep first thing next morning. Had I had high-altitude camping equipment this might have been a sensible plan.

Having slogged my way up usually in sunlight I was hot even in an open shirt and even at five o'clock, an hour before sunset. The high Andes offer no hint at all of the incredible drop in temperature that night brings, nor of how perplexingly fast the earth loses its warmth. An hour after nightfall the mountains can be fifty degrees colder than they were an hour before. Two hours after, the babbling stream is silenced and the bog would support a house.

I pitched tent on the levellest slope I could find. The bushes and flowers had been left far below. Here there was only grass, very short and coarse. I was against one side of the valley. The stream ran in a rocky gulley beside me.

While I was boiling water for porridge three little Quechua boys climbed up from the stream. They greeted me and stood in a line silently. I gave them a loaf of bread each. The loaves are small, flat and round; I had a big bagful of them for handing out on my walk. The boys were too shy to thank me.

Each of them wore a short poncho and short, black woollen trousers like those the Aymaras wear. They had colourful woolly hats with the earflaps. But they wore no socks; only open tyre-tread sandals. They stood with their mouths open, their eyes sparkling.

One of them said, 'Beng, senzor. Beng a la casa, senzor,' in a high, strident voice. He was not at all shy. He had just had nothing to say until now. He must have been to school, this one, to be able to invite me to his house in Spanish.

'Where is it?' I asked, because I was already exhausted.

'Cerquita,' he cried: very near. He pointed briefly up the valley, with a loose arm.

I looked, past the tent, to where he had pointed. There, a few hundred yards away, and a few hundred feet higher up, were two thatched adobe huts which I had failed to notice before, so well did they blend with the red rocks of the valley wall.

But I had pitched the tent, taken things out of my rucksack, had the porridge simmering—to pack everything away now and climb still further was an appalling prospect.

I said, 'Mañana.' Tomorrow.

'Frío,' the boy advised. 'Mucho frío.'

I waved confidently at my tent and sleeping bag.

The boys waited a while, not knowing what to do, or more likely fascinated by me and my strange camping things. Then they scampered up to their home.

Shadows were already creeping up hillsides in the distance. The valley filled with shadow, though the sky remained dazzling blue. For ten minutes the world stayed like this: very bright above, everything visible around me, but deep in a hazy gloom of twilight. Then suddenly, as if a door were being closed, to keep light out, the world became dark. Light vanished, evaporated. The world resumed its original condition. My kerosene stove hissed fiercely under the saucepan, and the blades of grass around it glowed, the only warm things in the Andes.

I slept little that night. I wore every piece of clothing I had: I wore my boots in my sleeping-bag. I lay freezing and still because when I turned I felt even colder.

The morning brought no relief. Sunlight touched the tops of the hills: it would be half an hour or more before it sank into my valley. The stream was choked with ice. Shivering and sleepless I began packing up the tent.

Then one of the Quechua boys was back. I had not noticed

him coming down from his house. He just appeared beside me.

'Beng a la casa, senzor,' he said. It was the one who had spoken last night.

'Gracias. Vámanos.' Let's go.

Far from refreshed, it was all I could do to reach their compound. The pass seemed an impossible proposition now.

On the way the boy said his mother had died from cold one night, and I believed him.

The boy's brothers and father were watching for my arrival. They stood looking down on me over the wall of their yard, and came to the gap in the wall to greet me when I had climbed up.

'Buen día,' said the father, a man in poncho and short trousers like his three sons. He looked at least fifty; but his sons were still boys: it was only the sun that had wrinkled his face. He laughed nervously, and repeated, 'Buen día.' I guessed, rightly, that the two words were the extent of his Spanish.

He led me into his yard. Three of its walls were formed by three thatched adobe houses. They had no windows. From one of them emerged an old woman in a dusty black dress. She brought a blanket and spread it out on the ground, bending down with her legs straight and apart to pull out the corners. She muttered as she did so, and smiled with the effort. She nodded and grinned and motioned me to sit down. I did, disappointed that I had not been asked inside: I was still freezing. But Quechua protocol prescribes that guests should be received in the yard. Indoors is regarded as too domestic and squalid.

The father stood beside me, chuckling and mumbling. The boys stood watching me from the other side of the yard. I looked at the one who spoke Spanish and called out: 'Is it the mother of your father?'

'Sí, sí, senzor,' the boy piped.

The father laughed quietly and nodded a long time.

The old woman, who had disappeared inside, came out again with a small piece of cloth, like the one she wore as a shawl, bundled up in her hands. She set it on the ground and unfolded it. There were ten little potatoes inside.

'Gracias, gracias.'

The father nodded and said something in Quechua. The woman retreated. I picked one up. He bent down and took one and leaning in front of me peeled it, to show me how: then nodded with his neck and shoulders as well as his head.

'Sí, señor,' I said, and skinned mine as he had done, pulling off the flaky skin with my nails. He put the one he had peeled back with the others, nearest me.

I alone sat and ate. They were good little potatoes, not the mealy but the viscous kind. But I was still frozen; the sun had not yet reached this little yard on a spur of the valley side.

I said to the boy: 'Frio. Muy frio.'

He made no reply. But the father obviously understood the word and repeated it—without making any of the usual gestures to suggest feeling cold. He simply said it. He was used to it by now.

I stood up and rubbed my arms and stamped the ground. Then I opened my bag and took out several loaves. I handed them to the father, who smiled and held them in front of him. I returned to my bag for tea-bags.

I had to get indoors to warm up. 'Can I make you tea?' I called to the boy.

He looked uneasily from me to his father. So I pulled out my pan too. The boy spoke in Quechua. The father took the pan and the tea-bags from me and went inside the cooking hut with his load.

I said, 'Can I go in?' pointing to the door. The boy was silent; then walked to the door and looked back at me; opened the door; turned round to me again; spoke to his father inside; the father came out and grinned; I signalled to enter; the father stood there and nodded—so I went in.

The cooking hut was a cramped womb of wood smoke. The fire, stoked under a clay mound covered with blackened pans, gave out a good heat. Through a small hole in the roof by which the smoke was meant to escape streamed a dense ray of sunlight, almost like a solid beam, so thick was the smoke it slatted. Yet even in here one was aware of the cold outside, of how small and frail a refuge was this hut.

The father had my pan over the fire. When the water boiled he dropped in the tea-bags and took it off the heat. Then he lifted the lid off one of the other big pans on the stove and spooned out a bowl of thin soup with chunks of potato. He passed it to me slowly, with both hands.

'Gracias, señor.'

He neither smiled nor nodded. He was more serious indoors.

I ate silently. I went to fetch my sugar, and also a postcard of downtown La Paz. I poured sugar into the pan, knowing the Indians have sweet teeth, and gave the card to the father, who stared at it for a while, cocking his head and turning it round.

The boy stood by his seated father to look too.

'Bolivia,' I said. 'La Paz.'

'Sí, sí,' said the boy. Then on the floor he drew four little circles side by side, with the end of a spoon. 'Cuzco. Bolivia. La Paz. Peru,' he explained, pointing to them one after another. He added two more on one end of his line: 'America. Inglaterra.'

'I'm from England,' I said.

'Sí,' he answered, as if he knew already.

The father poured out the tea into two large cups which I passed around. I began to feel well again, heated from within and without.

When I left, the family reassembled in the yard. The sun had reached it now, and was blinding. The father lifted his arm towards me like a lever with his fist closed. This is how the Indian men shake hands. You take hold of the closed hand for an instant, and let it drop. It is unsettling, a gesture on the man's part both of submission and of concealment.

'Buen día,' said the father.

'Adiós,' called his son, as I walked out of their yard.

Compared to the Aymaras, the Quechuas seem quiet, docile people. For much of their history they have acquiesced to authority from outside. Repeatedly they have been held by empires: by Tiahuanaco, by its offshoot Huari, by the Incas, by the Spaniards. Rather than resist it, they have accepted imperial might and bowed to it. They don't have the aggressiveness of the Aymaras; they don't fight one another, nor anyone else. They welcome strangers.

The pass, a saddle between the brows of two hills, brought me into a wide bowl in the mountains. Here the earth was red except where thin patches of grass had survived the grazing of alpacas. For even in this desolate basin almost 17,000 feet high, there was a little adobe hamlet whose inhabitants lived off potatoes and alpaca milk. Up on a hillside, beneath great fingers of bare rock, two young girls were driving along a herd of the white animals. Nearly all alpacas are white. They have thick, bushy fleeces above their spindly legs. Often their wool gets matted into slabs on their sides, or hangs down in solid chunks from their bellies, to be kicked by the hind legs as they walk.

I saw only one person in the village, an old woman who again spread out a blanket and brought potatoes.

Quechua hospitality to strangers is so customary that it comes with no sense of generosity. It is an obligation. If this woman had understood that I was thanking her, she would have wondered why. A widely known Quechua folk tale tells the story of an old man who arrives at a wedding feast like the ancient mariner. No one knows who he is. Most of the guests ignore him and continue their drinking and dancing and eating. But one couple seat him on the ground, bring food and drink, and listen to him. He tells them of an imminent disaster: a great fire is about to destroy the village. As soon as he has eaten, he leaves with the couple. They alone escape the destruction, because they were hospitable.

I had a second pass to face, on the far side of this bowl. As I climbed I looked back on the little village. All I could see of it was its rush-coloured roofs: the adobe walls were indistinguishable from the earth around them, of which they were made. Pacha Mama not only feeds, she also houses her people. It was bewildering to see that men lived there. Anywhere else in the world the earth would be deep under snow and ice at this altitude. Only in the dry, tropical air of the Andes is the snow-line so high. But even so, this desolate valley was such a remote, unwelcoming place to live: why did people ever come here, let alone settle here? Are the Quechuas happy in their solitude? Perhaps that's why they are so hospitable: they are content in the peaceful seclusion of the high mountains, and are happy to share what they count their good fortune.

But there are many bleak regions of the world where men have settled.

At the second pass there stood a little pile of stones, an *apachita*. The Aymaras have these too. They are shrines where people leave offerings to appease the mountain spirits who might otherwise make a journey fatal. Coca is the usual offering. The wild winds that swoop down on the high passes snatch away the leaves.

Then for the rest of the day I walked downhill along the turfy banks of a stream. Finally, in the late afternoon, I came out on a wide valley floor with a full river along one side, the Río Pitumarca. It was like returning to the world of men: the flat bed of the canyon was a green and sodden meadow, and the rocks of the valley walls were grey. I had left the red earth behind. And out in the middle of the meadow, among a flock of little cream-coloured things which were sheep, there sat three black heaps: Quechua women.

I walked out towards them. I wanted to ask them how far it was to the next village. Great puddles broke up the surface of the field. I had to walk in wide arcs to avoid them, and even so my boots sank deep into the soaked turf. It was like a flood meadow, set in the huge tank of a canyon.

The women sat quietly chewing coca, while their sheep munched the grass. These Quechuas wore the usual black dresses, but had wide, flat hats made of black velvet with braid around the edge. They would have looked at home in a bullring.

I said, 'Buenas tardes, señoras.'

The women were sitting on folded blankets. Only one of them looked up. 'Buenas,' she said so quietly it was almost a whisper. Her face was dirty.

By chance she spoke some Spanish, and told me it was two hours to Pitumarca, the next settlement down the river. Her companions muttered to one another. Hearing her say, 'Dos horas,' after a little pause, I knew it was only an estimate. She meant it felt like two hours of walking.

As I drew away I could hear the women's voices echoing in the canyon.

The valley closed in and my path swung high up on to one side among jagged spires and buttresses, a smooth path of dust beaten solid by centuries of feet and hooves. Night came upon me; at one end of the valley a curtain of colours, and at the other a huge, shaking moon which gave enough light to walk by. Boulders cast strong, liquid shadows on the ground. The mountains became intimate: they were mild, sleeping creatures now, not the unfriendly faces of the day.

Only in the middle of the next morning, after a good night's sleep, did I see Pitumarca. It was another hamlet, compact in a crook of the valley. It stood on a kind of natural bridge. A hundred yards upstream of it the river vanished into a tunnel, to re-emerge beyond the village.

I wound down to the dwellings. In one adobe yard a group of men and women were dancing. An old man stood to one side playing sampoña pipes. His tune was short and endlessly repeated: a pentatonic melody, shifting between the major and relative minor keys. Every so often he would pause for an instant, and then start again assertively and victoriously in the major key.

The dancers, in two rows of six, women in one and men in the other, would all stamp their feet in the piper's pause; then the men would lean down and mimic digging with a spade, and the women would twirl around on the spot, their black dresses swirling high sometimes to reveal their strong brown legs. All the dancers were barefoot on the earth.

For a long time they continued like this, digging and twirling. Then the men came weaving between the women, in a long snake from one end. Pairs were formed, and danced around one another, till every woman had taken a man's hand, and with a sudden stamp of their feet, all together, they stopped.

The old man continued his tune for a few notes, then realized the dance had finished. Briefly, indecisively, he stopped playing, but then started again, shuffling about as he piped, and rocking his torso in time to his music. If the tune was good a hundred times it was good for a few more. Two men made their way over to him, stomping and crying out, and danced with him. Everyone was in high spirits, whooping and laughing.

'Buenas,' one of the male dancers called to me, lifting his arm high.

I stood with my elbows on the adobe wall of the yard. He walked up to me. 'How was the dance?' he asked eagerly.

'Magnífico.'

'Eh,' he cried and burst out laughing and turned to look at his friends.

'The day after tomorrow,' he told me, 'we dance at Raqchi. At the Raqchi Dance Fiesta.'

'Sí?'

'Yesterday we danced at the competition in Sicuani. We passed. Saturday—Raqchi,' he said, full of awe for the great event. 'Do you know Raqchi?'

'No, señor.'

'There are groups from all over the Altiplano. Dance, dance, dance, all day.' His eyes glistened in the dry creases of their lids. 'The greatest fiesta of the year.'

This was obviously a fiesta I should not miss.

Next day I was back in the Vilcanota valley. A truck took me to Combapata, where I spent the rest of the day trying to find the schoolteacher to retrieve my belongings. Then I travelled on to Raqchi.

10

DANCES

IT IS NIGHT. The moon has not yet risen. When it does, it will be full. Ahead, on the far side of the meadow I am crossing, scattered lamps show up a cluster of sheet and sackcloth tents; the occasional pole protruding erratically out into the night catches a glint of light. It could be a hastily pitched nomads' camp. Beyond it, a patch of murky white hovers dimly: the church. I cannot see it, but over that dark rise must be the village of Raqchi.

The tents form a rough-hewn crystal in the night. Night is thrown back around them. I enter one, a bright shelter from the dark, in search of supper. By the entrance stands a large, crude stove, top-heavy with huge saucepans. Within, pots and bowls and plates of food cooked and uncooked litter tables, chairs and ground, so it is difficult to take a step. A woman and her daughter and husband are all busy preparing

155

more food, to the rush of the stove's flames. There is a second cooker inside, hidden by a great wide frying pan at which the mother is frying meat.

She is a young Chola, plump but unwrinkled. She is not wearing her hat. She has a severe pallid parting, the hair stretched flat either way into her two long black plaits.

'Buenas noches, gringo,' she calls out. 'What do you want? Meat? Soup? There's steak, stew, fried chicken with fried potatoes, chicken with rice. Qué quiere?'

'Where are you from?' breaks in her daughter, a girl of ten or twelve, bright and quick as the children often are, unlike their parents.

'De Inglaterra,' I tell her.

'Ah,' she says, and repeats the word: 'Inglatyerra.'

Then with an imploring frown she asks: 'Why don't you take me to your country?'

I say to the mother: 'Can I take her?'

She turns over a huge slab of steak, amid a wild chorus of hissing in the pan, and replies: 'Of course. And me too. I'll come to live in your country.'

'It's ugly,' I warn her. 'The sun never shines.'

'Aiee,' she screams. Then: 'I don't believe it. Inglatyerra is much more beautiful than Peru.'

The daughter clears a table, putting all the bowls and pans on the ground beside it. The mother gives me steak and chips. All the while her husband works over in a dim corner of the tent, slicing meat from a hung side of llama.

These were Cholos, all these people who had brought their tents and kitchens to Raqchi. Most of them had come from Sicuani, the nearest town, and it was not only for business that they were here. They were as excited about the dancing as any of the Quechuas. There would be Cholo groups dancing tomorrow too: dancing is one area of life in which the Cholos have maintained their older traditions. But tonight it was the food that mattered, and all the tents were hives of chopping and frying and boiling and tasting.

After supper, when I told the woman I was going to camp

156

in the meadow she gave me blankets despite my protesta-
tions. 'It's cold in a tent,' she informed me.

Over by the bank which closed off the meadow there was a
group of small camping tents flickering with heavy shadows
cast by a fire they surrounded. I made for them. It was a
Peruvian Boy Scout troop. They had roped themselves off a
corner of the field.

Their leader, the only one not in uniform, rose when I
appeared behind the ring of boys seated round the fire. He
was delighted to have me pitch tent within their enclosure. I
should come and join them once I was settled.

But I had other plans. There were ruins here, beyond the
rise of the meadow. I climbed it: and suddenly was facing a
transformed world. The moon had risen and hung, a fat lamp,
a few inches above the horizon. Before it the land had become
layer upon layer of receding blue which finally merged with a
luminous sky. And standing a hundred yards away was a
massive row of black giants linked arm in arm.

It was the Temple of Viracocha. This ruin is nothing more
than a wall; but at fifty feet high it is the tallest structure the
Incas ever built. There used to be pillars running along either
side of it. These supported a roof halfway up: so there would
have been open shelter on both sides. Now only the bases of
the pillars remain, no more than circles of rubble on the
ground. But the holes in the wall where the roof beams would
have lain are open; and underneath each of them is a tall, thin
doorway. These gaps, evenly spaced a few yards apart all
along the 300-foot length of the wall, divide it into sections:
and make the sections look like huge warriors holding one
another, as if the structure were a vast sheet of paper folded
up, cut in the right places, and opened out again as a string of
men. And with the moonlight coming from behind, the wall
was so deep a black against the blue world that it could almost
have been a shape cut out of the background revealing the
lightless void beyond. It was unearthly.

The eighth Inca emperor, Inca Viracocha, built the temple.
His father, Yahuar Huacac, was a weak and ineffectual ruler.

He had done nothing to expand the Incas' territory, which at that time did not extend beyond the valley of Cuzco, from which the Incas originated. Yahuar had been taken hostage as a child by the Ayarmacas, who inhabited the Vilcanota valley, this region, because his mother should have been given to them in marriage to fulfill a contract of wife-exchanging opened some generations before. The Ayarmacas therefore considered that her child would rightly have been theirs, and so kidnapped him. They kept him several years; then sent him back. Many years later, when Yahuar Huacac was Inca, his son had a dream, or so the legend goes. In the dream the creator god, the supreme Inca divinity Viracocha, appeared to Yahuar's son and warned him that an army from a valley in the west was advancing on Cuzco. When the young man awoke he told his father of his dream. Yahuar advised him to ignore it. It was just a dream.

But the pious and brave youth ignored his father's scepticism. If his father wouldn't call up the army, then he would raise his own. He went out towards the alleged aggressors, gathering forces from among the alpaca- and llama-herding population on his way. (Or as the legend goes, he went with a small band of shepherds.) Sure enough, there was a hostile army advancing on Cuzco. He fell upon them in a surprise attack and defeated them.

Elated by victory and the divine favour in which he evidently stood, he returned gloriously to Cuzco to depose his own father, declare himself Inca, and bestow on himself the name Viracocha. Riding high on his triumph, he marched southwards from Cuzco with the full army along the Vilcanota valley, and conquered the Ayarmacas who had imprisoned his father. So the Incas' route to Lake Titicaca was opened up. Thereafter their expansion began in earnest. It was the early fifteenth century. Fifty years later they held the greatest empire in the New World; and in another half-century that empire had fallen into the hands of a small band of Spaniards.

Inca Viracocha built his temple at Raqchi after subduing the Ayarmacas. It was a monument to the start of the Inca

expansion. But he had it raised in honour of the god Viracocha: a massive token of gratitude to the god for deigning to
visit a young man in his sleep. It was built for the Inca's
dream.

Why so tall? Why unlike any other Inca structure?

When I returned the scout leader, his mestizo face a bronze
mask in the firelight, gave the only answer: 'Quién sabe?'

In the morning sun the giants stand less strangely on the
cold, wet ground: they are just a wall after all. The illusion
has shut itself up like a perverse flower at the paling of the
sky. On the other side of the bank, in the meadow, a wooden
stage has been erected near the Cholo tents. No doubt it was
already there last night and I failed to see it in the dark.
Beside it stands a pole on which two megaphones have been
fastened, ready to announce the start of the dance fiesta.

The meadow is seething with people: Cholos, Quechuas,
white Peruvians, foreigners—for this fiesta is advertised in
Cuzco and some of the tourists are driven down to it. The
crowds are seated on the banks around the meadow, and
catch the sun like ants. The only empty space is the stage
itself, a blank square waiting to be filled. The Cholo tents rise
out of the mass like pale rocks. The Scouts' enclave is surrounded by spectators. The air, too, is filled now, by a voice
blaring from the megaphones. Screeching and distorted and
incomprehensible, it assaults the ear. But you can tell it is
building slowly up to a climax, which it reaches: and a troupe
of children in brilliant, clean Quechua clothes scurries up
steps on to the stage as a band of pipes, guitars and drums
strikes up. It is the first dance of the day.

Even over the megaphones the music is strongly rhythmic.
The drummer thumps out a galloping beat; the guitars come
across less clearly, their chords sounding more like a continuous hum—they are not quite in tune, and the players don't
allow enough space between the beats; but the pipe-players
are professionals. They are playing keña flutes: long straight
flutes made of wood, primitive recorders. (In fact, the making

159

of the folkloric instruments, though it continues rough and ready in the countryside, has also moved into the cities, where skilled mestizo craftsmen make special pipes and flutes and charangas for the professional Andean bands.) The band is sitting just behind the stage. There are three or four flute-players. Their melody works its way up and down the scale, bright and clear and exciting, in the major key yet with that pentatonic sense of ambivalence, of almost being in the minor key too, returning every few bars.

The children have formed two rows up on the stage. The girls are wearing short black dresses and heavily embroidered shirts and the wide black hats. All the clothes are new, the colours clean and strong: red, green and gold.

The girls are turning from side to side, on the spot: six girls spinning back and forth in a line. With every swirl their dresses fan out and you can see their whole bodies as one straight thing, from their swinging hair down to their bare brown legs. All the girls have an astonishing natural grace-fulness. They are taken completely by the rhythm of the dance, and somehow the rhythm gives them an ease of move-ment that you would hardly expect from the most accom-plished dancers. They have a flowing grace; they seem to be perfect, mature women, easy and elegant at once. Yet none of these girls is older than ten. As they swirl round and round, their skirts billowing out, their limbs move in precise time to the music. With their tilting hips, shuffling feet and with their ankles twisting a little as their bare feet turn on the floor, they seem so self-assured, so genuinely confident and inde-pendent; as if, instinct with rhythm, they are quite unper-turbed by the huge crowd watching them. And because they are self-enclosed, because they seem to want nothing, be-cause they merely stay where they are, swinging their hips and flexing their knees, it is the boys who come seeking them.

The boys, in blazing Quechua clothes, bright choro hats, colourful ponchos, clean short white trousers, stomp the wooden stage with their bare feet, stepping back and forth in front of the girls. Their movements are taut, their trousered legs lifting and dropping almost mechanically, not at all forced. For as their feet come down they bend their knees making their bodies drop too; they seem to push their feet down into the floor with every step, their bodies sinking and rising, sinking and rising to the music. And though they are moving about in front of the girls, they are not showing off to them. There is neither arrogance nor pride in their movements. They are engrossed in their own dancing.

Then the boys come weaving among the girls, in and around and out from the line of girls who swing and swirl and shuffle just as before, as if the boys weren't there, flowers that have attracted bees, who bring them pollen. Finally, after circling his girl many times, each boy takes her hand, and the pairs are formed. Then again in two rows, each opposite his chosen. In its turn each pair passes right through between the two rows, from end to end, consummating their union: now boy and girl dance round one another, hand in hand. The act of life is fulfilled. One by one the pairs dance their way off the stage, until the square is left empty again.

Before the emptiness of the stage has ceased to be striking another troupe of twelve, six men and six women, has come dancing up on to it. They are dressed exactly as the children were; they are adult versions of the same people. Their dance is similar to the first. It tells the same story, of love and procreation, as do many of the day's dances, for they are all dances acting out the facts of life. Folk dancing, like primitive art, doesn't reflect life so much as the basic principles of life. These men move with the same tautness as the boys did, but with more precision and better synchronized. But there is still something boyish about the tight lifting and dropping of the limbs and in the rigid, rhythmic movements. Even these men seem humble beside the women, who spin so self-assuredly, knowing the men will come to them. Perhaps the women have less of the supple grace of the girls, but they make up for it with a litheness in their limbs that comes from the stiffening and filling out of the body as it grows and strengthens. These women are mothers.

So throughout the day the dances continue. There are groups from all over southern Peru and northern Bolivia, but nearly all perform dances which tell the same story. The crowd becomes more fluid, not used to watching so many dances on a stage: usually they participate themselves. What was at first exciting, to see well-known steps performed so well in front of a fieldful of spectators, becomes rather tedious and artificial for the Cholos and Quechuas watching. A dance is best done in the middle of a drunken crowd at a fiesta; not as a show. Gradually the field thins as the Indians wander into the Chola women's tents for food. The vendors up on the bank around the meadow become thronged.

Especially the *chicha*-sellers. They have big plastic jugs and buckets of their brew, into which they dip glasses for their customers. Chicha, a thick, sweet, cream-coloured beer, is made from maize. Women chew the corn and spit it into buckets in which it ferments. It is the Quechuas' favourite drink.

But I can't take my eyes off the dancing. In the afternoon there is more variety, the dances are more specific and light-hearted. In one a boy wears a horned mask and charges among a troupe of dancing men who try to catch him. In another, all the men carry hobby-horses and wear wide-brimmed hats. These are dances about the Spaniards, who brought horses and bullfights to the New World. By playfully enacting the Spanish customs, the Indians keep themselves distinct, and even though these dances mark a change from the pre-Columbian forms, they must help to preserve the Indian way of life. But there is one dance, the dance of the Canchis who are Quechuas from high in the Eastern Cordillera, that stands out from all the rest.

The music starts up and is immediately arresting. No guitars, only the lonely sampoña pipes blown slow and deep in a minor key. The players are using their largest pipes, which spread from a foot long at one side of the sets to a yard at the other. I can see their heads tilting as they reach to play the heavy low notes. On these deepest tones you can almost hear the breaths of the musicians whistling faintly above the resonant music. A drum thuds at the start of every bar. There's nothing more: just the breathing pipes and the slow drum, and the great space between the two sounds. Suddenly you are reminded of the loneliness of the Andes, of the mountains' emptiness. The other dances say nothing of this: but here is the Quechuas' environment. Not just life, but life where it happens.

The six of each sex have come on to the stage. The men are holding long flutes to their mouths. They swoop slowly down and round with them, as if playing. Perhaps originally the dancers did play their own music in this one; maybe they still do when they perform in their own village. For this dance is only complete with this piece of music. In the others, any music with the right rhythm would do. But here, where the melody and the movements are so similar in mood, the two obviously go together.

The men wear huge plumed hats that fan up and out in a blaze of dyed feathers. They are like great waving crowns, asserting the importance of man's mind. Here, among the mountains, where mankind is dwarfed by the environment, human consciousness and significance need to be affirmed. Pacha Mama has to be reminded that she has people; as she is in this dance. In the others the important thing was to break free from the oppression of the land: at fiestas, where the dances are normally performed, the Indians can forget the harshness of their lives in the highlands, so their dances are fun. But not in this one.

The women hold short lengths of brightly-coloured rope between their hands. They swing them, both arms travelling up and round and down, so the colours shine above their heads and then in front. They sway their hips slowly from side to side, and then twist round. The men come in a long line among the women, weaving between them, but with none of the lively rhythm of the other dances. Here the men are sombre, solemn figures moving hypnotically between the women. Down they swoop with their flutes and crowns, then up, their torsos tilting either way. They seem for once dominating rather than boyish. They could be sorcerers weaving their spell among women; they could be acting our the part of the environment itself, the binding power of the land working its way among the people. The women swirl gently round and round, submissive. For even their colourful ropes are finally a bond, restricting the movement of each arm. In other dances, arms swing open and free, independent of one another. Here they are held together. Despite the brilliant colours of the men's feathers and the women's fetters, this dance finally speaks of the oppressive land: everything is constrained by the pact with Pacha Mama. When the pairs form and dance their way off the stage it seems that not only has the general truth of the sexes been revealed, but also the harshness of life in the high mountains. When the stage is empty the crowd is silent for a moment. The air above seems to echo the dance, for briefly a sadness hangs in the air. Whatever all the other dances may have affirmed, this one has revealed that the Quechuas are a sad people. Their world is desolate.

The next dance after the Canchis was yet another act about life. I had seen enough now, and I had a long way to go today: I wanted to reach Cuzco by night.

All day the Scouts had had sentries posted around their enclosure, so my tent and belongings were just as I left them that morning. I packed up and left.

The main road from Titicaca to Cuzco was only half a mile away. By good fortune there was a lorry parked at the side of the road. The driver was just climbing into the cab when I caught him: 'Señor! A Cuzco?'

'Sí,' he said once he had shut his door and wound down his window. 'Five hundred soles.'

He knew it was too much, and so did I. But he was adamant. Perhaps he thought there would be no other traffic from Raqchi that day, and had the monopoly. He may have been right.

I accepted. I was alone in the back. I stood up at the front looking over the cab and fat protuberant bonnet at the dirt road winding along beside the cement-coloured Vilcanota. It was late afternoon. Every half hour we passed under an avenue of shivering eucalyptus trees protecting an adobe and tin village. Night came.

The first I saw of Cuzco was a black hillside ahead studded with lights. Then we bumped up on to tarmac and the lorry was suddenly humming smoothly along. We speeded up. The lights in front reached out and drew us into a long trail of street-lamps.

It was midnight when I walked into the Plaza de Armas, the very heart of the Inca Empire.

11

THE NAVEL

AT A PLACE called Paccari Tampu, somewhere in southern Peru, there are three caves alongside one another. When the earth was unpeopled, four brothers and four sisters—though who their mother and father were is not known—stepped from the cave in the middle. From the caves on either side emerged ten bands of men and women, each band an *ayllu*, a lineage. One of the four brothers was Manco Capac, Rich in Virtues. He it was who led his siblings and the ten *ayllus* on a long journey. He was a pioneer, seeking a fertile home for his people. He wandered long enough for his brothers to die before he finally came over the brow of a hill and saw before him a valley, watered, wide and flat: here his people would settle. He called it the Navel, Cuzco, because it would be the centre of their world.

So runs one version of the story. Another relates that Manco

Capac arose from the waters of Lake Titicaca. As he stood on the shore, Viracocha, the creator god, came to him with a golden dagger. 'Where you can drive the blade into the earth,' said Viracocha, 'there you shall found a great city. Take this dagger, and seek the place.' And so began the wandering of Rich in Virtues, King Arthur's curious New World counterpart. It was a formidable task, to dig at all the Andes, or perhaps he was something of a dowser, guided by powers to the right place; but finally, in a wide, fertile valley, Manco stabbed the earth and found the dagger wrested from his hand and swallowed by the soil. It sank without trace. Manco had reached the promised land, the Navel of the world. And so he named the place.

Manco Capac married his sister, Mamo Ocllo. She bore him a son, Sinchi Roca, the very first pure Inca. Like the Pharaohs, the Inca monarchs had to have undiluted royal blood in their veins: only an Inca and his sister could produce an Inca. Meanwhile the ten *ayllus*, who were to become Inca nobility, not royalty, grew, and the settlement at the Navel became a flourishing community. The supreme Incas succeeded one another, and the fourth, Mayta Capac, ruled so vigorous a people that he was able to enlarge their territory. By now the Inca population was not alone in the world. When Mayta took over more lands in the valley he had first to subjugate the villagers who cultivated them. Mayta Capac's son and grandson, in their times as Inca, subjugated other villages nearby, and some in the valleys neighbouring the Navel. From them they took women as concubines. But it was only when the eighth Inca, the one who called himself Viracocha, ruled that the armies of the Navel began to venture further afield.

But the Incas weren't the only kingdom seeking to expand. To the west, the Chancas had become a powerful dynasty; far in the north of Peru, the Chimus held extensive territory and had built the world's largest city of mud on the Pacific shore; to the south were the Ayarmacas, already subjugated, and beyond them the long-established Colla and Lupaca kingdoms around Lake Titicaca. The ninth emperor, Pachacuti

Inca Yupanqui, He Who Overturns the Earth, succeeded by cunning diplomacy in diverting the hostile Chancas from attacking the Navel, and instead persuaded them to embark on a joint campaign with Inca forces to conquer the north. The forces became divided, ultimately, and the Incas took the important northern town of Cajamarca for themselves. The Chancas remained a dangerous foe: they conquered the Lupaca of Titicaca, and now threatened the Incas from west and south. But Pachacuti had already won the allegiance of a large population near the Navel, the Quechuas. With their numbers swelling the Inca armies, he embarked on two successive campaigns which were to win the Incas most of the great empire: first he went south, and conquered not only the Colla and Lupaca but the whole Titicaca basin; then he marched north to consolidate his hold over what had already been taken, and to press on all the way to Quito, capital of modern Ecuador. From here he was able to outflank the Chimu forces. In the course of his campaigns he subdued the Chancas. When he returned to the Navel the Incas held an empire reaching over three thousand miles from the northern Andes to the southern. He called it Tawantinsuyu, the Four Corners. As far as he knew, his dominions did indeed reach to the four corners of the earth.

But Pachacuti's son Topa pushed the corners still wider. After suppressing a Lupaca uprising he campaigned across the Altiplano and into Argentina and Chile. Then he made his way north, to sack the great Chimu mud city of Chan Chan. Meanwhile his administrators built the great roads of the Empire, the highways leading out from the Navel to north, south, east and west. They built tunnels and bridges and stairways in the mountainsides; every four miles along the road they erected tambos, rest-houses with storerooms; they manned these with their fastest runners, who in relays could take messages from the Navel to anywhere in the Four Corners within ten days. They built massive terraces on hillsides with good soil. They built irrigation systems. They built granaries where villagers were to store their surplus produce in time of plenty for time of need. They organized the whole population of the Empire into groups of ten families, these into groups of one hundred families, then five hundred, then a thousand, and ten thousand. They appointed governors at each decimal level so that they had a hierarchy of administrators reaching down by degrees from the Inca himself not just to the village headman, but to the head of every ten families. They resettled whole villages according to labour shortages, and to mix loyal subjects among rebellious, both as informers and as examples of happy compliance to the imperial administration. Rather than levying taxes they made their subjects work certain numbers of days each year in the fields set aside for the Incas' granaries. They ensured that all were adequately clothed and sheltered and fed. They made Quechua the universal language of the Empire. Pachacuti and his son did overturn the earth: they drastically changed life in the Andes.

Within three generations the Incas had grown from a dynasty in a small valley in the south of Peru to the rulers of the four corners of the earth. But the wheel of fortune turns in the New World too. Within another three generations the Incas had lost their Empire to the Spanish conquistadors. Once the Spaniards had seized the Navel, the Incas never regained it. Their god, Viracocha, would not forgive his people for allowing the centre of the world to be taken by infidels. He had grated them Cuzco, and they had lost it.

Cuzco is said to have been laid out in the form of a jaguar. At one end stood the massive fortress of Sacsayhuaman with its three serrated walls: these were the jaguar's teeth. The streets and building mapped out the rest of the beast. If this was true, Cuzco has been reshaped since the Spanish Conquest and no longer has a particular design. But one thing has not changed in the city's layout: Haucaypata, which was the great central square of Cuzco in Inca times, is still the centre of Cuzco. Now it is called the Plaza de Armas.

Coricancha, the great Inca temple of sun-worship, used to stand here. The Spaniards knocked it down and raised a cathedral instead. All around the central square were the royal palaces of the Incas. These were huge stone houses enclosing courtyards and fields: each palace had its own land. The design was based on the typical adobe village compound. Also in the centre of Cuzco was the palace of the royal virgins. This was the Inca equivalent of a nunnery. The girls served in worship in the Coricancha. From these virgins, once they had grown up and had spent sufficient time in religious duties, the Inca chose his concubines. They also had their palace, a vast harem filled with hundreds of women. When they were too old to please the Inca they returned to their homes as honourable citizens, the pride and envy of their families and former friends. None of the glorious palaces survived the Spanish Conquest intact. The Plaza de Armas is now, almost entirely, a European square.

In the morning after arriving in Cuzco I went down to the Plaza for breakfast. It was crammed with people. Along one side runs an arcade. In it sat hundreds of Chola women selling little items of food: pastries, stuffed peppers, potatoes, lumps of sweet fried dough. Between the seated women milled throngs of people. Out in the square itself, an open space hemmed by colonial buildings and patterned with little hedges, was a seething crowd. I had arrived in Cuzco, by good fortune, for the Fiesta of Corpus Christi.

This fiesta is one of the four in the year for which Quechuas who live in villages in the Province of Cuzco came into the city itself. There were hordes of them in the Plaza. On two sides of the square rows of trestle tables had been set up, on which Chola women had laid out platefuls of food: those were full meals. They sold the same dish: roast guinea pig with fried potatoes, and lettuce. Guinea pigs, which scurry about the yards and kitchens of Andean homes along with the hens and dogs and cats, are a speciality eaten only at fiestas. Skinned and cooked they are less than half as fat as when alive.

I bought one for a late breakfast. The Chola handed me a plateful and a spoon. 'Gringo,' she said. 'Have some *aji*.'

'No, gracias.' *Aji* is a tasteless but blindingly hot sauce made from the thin papery kind of red peppers.

The woman, hatless and wearing a thick emerald cardigan, opened her mouth and laughed. Her teeth were dappled with brown rot. She turned to the woman standing at the next table and they both laughed. The Cuzco Cholas are used to gringos.

For a while I stood there holding the plate in one hand and vainly prodding at the thin brown corpse with the spoon in my other. I wondered if it might really be a rat. The spoon was useless. So I picked up the little pig and chewed at it. Shreds of meat stuck with match-sized bones came away. The taste was good, somewhere between chicken and pork, but it was impossible to have a real mouthful and the bones were too big to crunch but small enough to be fiddly. It was an unsatisfying meal.

The cathedral occupies most of one side of the square. On the wide pavement in front of it sat three large circles of Quechuas. All the men were in grey-brown ponchos and black wool trousers, the women all wearing the wide black braid and velvet hats. Most had little pieces of cloth in their laps from which they picked roasted corn kernels. No one spoke. They all sat munching corn with their mouths open, chomping, their hands reaching into their laps every few seconds. The susurrus they produced was like horses eating.

Until one of the brass bands standing behind them suddenly started playing. In fact, it was one solitary trumpeter, in Quechua clothes, who decided that the time had come for music. His eyes half-closed and his cheeks drawn tight by a permanent smile of drunkenness, he lifted his battered instrument to his lips and simply blew. People who have never played before and want to have a go do as he did. He blew as hard and as loud as he could, one long note broken only when he needed to draw breath. Then he fiddled with the valves, pressing different combinations as he blasted. This distorted the note, rather than changing it. Meanwhile the other players had followed his lead. Two euphoniums and four trumpets joined in. And the bass-drummer, standing next to his drum with one hand on top to hold it steady, began to flog his rhythm out very confidently, as if there really were a melody that the band were playing, when in fact there was only the sizzle that brass instruments produce when blown hard enough. In the blaring noise it was possible to detect notes changing, but no two players ever changed notes at the same time. On the drum was written: 'Comunidad de Pisac— Provincia de Cuzco': these Quechuas had come from Pisac, then, a village in the next valley, and were presumably a regular band.

The corn-munchers sat just as before, jaws moving up and down, lips drawn back, even though the bells of the trumpets were pointed straight at them from a few feet away.

Then the other brass band, which boasted a trombonist, began to blast too. The point, evidently, was to make noise, and the two bands were therefore not competing with one another. Even if they had been playing recognizable and mutually conflicting tunes, it would still have been a joint effort: to fill the air with noise. No one seemed to mind, or even to notice. The Quechuas chomped on, oblivious to all but the taste of the corn, and the crowds continued to throng close by.

The Plaza de Armas slopes gently from one end to the other. Cuzco is built on the side of a hill. From the upper end I could see the faded green hills across the wide Cuzco valley. Up here there were more vendors hidden among the multitude, but of a kind I hadn't seen before: gringos.

Mexicans who wanted the khaki-uniformed American troops out of their country used to chant 'Green, go,' meaning: uniforms, out. From this came the term gringo, now used throughout Latin America to refer to whites. But since the hippie movement sent emissaries into South America in the early Seventies, the word has acquired a secondary meaning. To ordinary gringos like me there was a breed of real gringos whose capital is Cuzco. They are hippies, they take organic drugs, eat wholesome food to counteract the ill-health the drugs produce, and they wear Indian clothes and accessories, which they are beginning to make themselves; and to sell. They sit up at the top end of the square, men and women, in ponchos, besides sheets of velvet on which they lay out the native-inspired jewellery which they fashion in their hotel rooms. Most have the odd tool by their feet—pliers, a file, a sheet of emery paper—to suggest the authenticity of their works: the big round copper earrings are of a pre-Columbian design, but they were genuinely made by a gringo craftsman.

I went up one of the steep stepped lanes which climb from the Plaza de Armas. The houses on either side were small whitewashed Spanish dwellings with dark wooden doors. Soon the noise of the plaza was left behind.

I came to a small bar, an open door to mark it. Inside there was a formica-topped counter and three square formica tables. Apart from barman, there were only six customers, all Cuzqueños in ordinary western clothes. They were mestizos, grouped around one table cluttered with brown beer bottles. All turned to look when I came in. I sat at the nearest table; their babble of talk gradually resumed.

The barman, a weary Spaniard with white hair, a heavily lined forehead and an impish expression on his face, raised his eyebrows at me. When I didn't respond he said: 'Qué?'

'Café con leche,' I called.

He turned away slowly, allowing his eyes to glance round the room.

The mestizos were talking loudly about Peru, rarely letting a man speak alone. One said that the country was too big: they should never have annexed half of Ecuador's jungle, for the jungle was useless yet cost a great deal of military expense to hold. Another simultaneously said, 'But the oil, the oil.'

'If there is oil in the jungle, then we've already got enough of it.'

'The more the better. It's logical.'

'You have your profits, true. But you have your expenses too. And the Indians in the jungle, what do we do with them?'

'In that part of the jungle there are no Indians.'

'Yes there are. They have already killed two engineers.'

'I don't believe it. They died accidental deaths.'

'No. It has been confirmed.'

The barman came out from behind the counter with a steel tray. With a slow, steady hand he set on the table a glass of hot milk, a spoon and a glass jug of black coffee with a metal lid.

'Cincuenta solitos, no más,' he said: fifty little soles, no more.

I gave him the money: less than tenpence. He walked away.

I poured the thick, strong coffee into the milk. There was only room in the glass to make the milk pale brown. When I had drunk down I strengthened the colour.

I sat quietly, hoping to avoid the inevitable attention of the drunk mestizos. Soon enough it came: 'Eh! Eh!'

I ignored the call.

'Eh! Gringo.'

I had to look: all six of them were staring at me. One scraped his chair to the side to open me up to the full view of all at the table.

Mesitzos have Indian faces: swarthy, high-cheeked, tight-eyed. But they usually grow mustaches to show that they can: Indians are bald except for their heads of hair. And the skin of mestizos wrinkles in smaller, thinner creases than the tough Indian skin, which rather folds.

One, with a small moustache of black and grey hairs, asked me: 'What do you think of Peru?' He was staring at me, but with some effort: his eyes glistened with drink.

'Very good.'

'And Cuzco?' The others were silent.

'Very good.' They all nodded.

'And how long have you been here?'

'Only today.'

'Did you come for the Inti Raymi?' asked a young man with a heavy drooping moustache.

'What?'

'El Inti Raymi. The fiesta this afternoon. You haven't heard of Inti Raymi? It was the biggest Inca fiesta. The Festival of the Sun. *Inti* is the sun, and *raymi* is a fiesta. In Quechua.'

'It still takes place?'

'Sí, sí. This afternoon, because today is the summer solstice. In the fortress of Sacsayhuaman. But it's very famous.'

'You mean the *campesinos'*—the polite word for Indians— 'still perform an Inca ceremony?' I asked.

'Sí, sí,' replied the young man. 'Bueno, they're not all *campesinos* who take part. There are some actors. It's a show for the tourists. But it's very, very authentic, exactly as the fiesta used to be when the Incas celebrated it. You must see it.'

The others agreed. Then a thin old man with white hair razored bristle-short said: 'But really, is Peru a beautiful country? Truthfully.'

'It's the most beautiful country I ever visited,' I lied. I had been asked this question, and the next, in every bar I had entered so far in Peru where there had been a mestizo drinking.

Another broke in: 'But fraternally—we are all men, we are all brothers: you and me, we are brothers on this earth—how do the Peruvians seem to you? We have big problems in this nation—but what do you think of us Peruvians?'

The sudden boom of a drum, and another, and another. Its beat has started and will continue relentlessly. A fast beat, perfectly regular, faster than a march: a run. This is the rhythm for Inti Raymi. Then come the flutes: a falling theme, played again, falling down, and again. It is endlessly repeated, unchanging, like the drumbeat thumping underneath.

Out into the open square comes a great platoon of warriors, running out. They wear loincloths, bearing spears. They run out in step to take their place to one side of the stage that has been erected in the middle of the open space; they keep their square formation, running on the spot, bare feet beating the earth in time with the drum and flute.

Then another platoon wearing tunics comes running out to the other side of the stage. Now the square formed by the crowd of spectators is half-filled with running men, all in time with one another. The warriors are on two sides of the stage, but in front: beyond the stage is the other half of the arena, empty, save for five pyres of straw waiting to be lit.

Then out come two groups, not warriors but sacred: a band of virgins and a band of young priests, both running out in step with the whole field of warriors, so everyone is running to the one infectious beat. The whole mass of people in the arena stomp the ground with one rhythm. It is like the running creatures on the Gate of the Sun at Tiahuanaco: they were all running to the sun in the centre of the lintel. Here, the people are running for the sun, the supreme force ordering the Inca Empire.

Suddenly the music stops. All the runners—virgins, priests and warriors—stand still. For a moment there is silence. A new theme starts on flute and drum, slow, melancholy, more religious. Now and then comes the hollow blowing of conch shells. Messengers stand at the side of the arena holding the shells to their mouths. The mass of people sways, everyone swaying from side to side, slowly, to the music. This continues a long time. Then it stops, and all is still: the Inca himself has arrived.

Two sweepers come out into the arena; the mass of people has drawn into two to make a gangway. The sweepers, stooping and sweeping with bunches of twigs the ground the Inca will pass over, move towards the stage itself, which has been painted to look like a stone altar. Behind them follow two rows of high priests in feather headdresses and long robes, and behind them, the Inca himself in his litter, which is set down a little way before the altar. Everyone in the arena bows down, all kneel and lie forwards, heads down, arms outstretched. The Inca raises himself and walks to the stage, and up the steps on to it, between the two rows of motionless high priests. A man has been pressing close behind him, carrying a huge shade on a long pole high over the Inca's head; but now he makes his solitary way back to the litter while the Inca, on stage, raises his arms to the sun. All the people sing now, a simple pentatonic tune. The Inca and one of the high priests prepare a bowl of liquid which they pour into an earthen jar at the head of the stage. The singing stops and the Inca makes a speech, addressing the sun with imploring gestures. The hierarchy of the religion is plain: warriors, virgins, priests, high priests, the Inca: everyone there to worship the sun, but the Inca the pinnacle of the populace, the only one who actually addresses the sun.

Then the drum is off again, with that first running rhythm. Suddenly the whole arena is set in motion. The virgins are swinging their hips and waving rainbow-coloured flags; all the warriors stand on the spot tapping one foot on the ground. Then with long strides four small groups of spear-bearers come leaping forwards, out to where the pyres are. One of them has a torch, and sets all five pyres alight. The spear-bearers withdraw. Then a llama is released into the arena; it looks about, confused. But already a group of young priests swinging ropes around above their heads has come out stalking the animal. They come closer and closer. It is a tame llama: one takes hold of it and tethers it to a stake. The priests dance round and round the llama, the beat of the drum getting faster and faster, the priests running closer and closer, the llama looking about frantically, not knowing which way to stand. But suddenly three of the priests have leapt on the beast and pulled it to the ground. They tie up its legs and leave it lying there while virgins come within the circle of dancing priests and make their own inner circle, dancing round the llama.

The llama is carried to the stage where one of the high priests kneels beside it, raises a dagger above his head, and actually stabs the animal to death, cutting open the hide and flesh of the whole belly so he can get in with his knife and cut free the animal's heart, which he pulls out still hot, probably still throbbing, blood all over his arms, and raises towards the sun. Then he comes off the stage and puts the heart on the largest pyre. The music has stopped and all in the arena are prostrate. This is the climax of the ceremony, the people's offering to the sun. The Aymaras bury llama foetuses, symbols of fertility, for Pacha Mama; the Incas burned llama hearts, symbols of life, for the sun.

Sun-worship was a religion which matched the order of Inca society: a supreme deity to be revered above all others; and a supreme ruler, a hierarchy of lesser governors beneath him. So well did the religion and political structure fit one another, in fact, that they were not distinct: the Inca himself was both ruler and highest priest; his high priests were his highest administrators; the governors in the provinces were expected to officiate in ceremonies of sun-worship. The Inca, as highest priest, was in closer contact with the sun, and this reinforced his authority: the religion was both a pattern and a tool for the state.

Yet the Incas tolerated every superstition of their subjects. They did almost nothing to impose sun-worship on the mass of the Empire's population. In many cases they encouraged local beliefs and religious practices by venerating idols and shrines themselves. But this was a strategy: they would insist that an idol deserved to be housed in some nearby Inca temple: the idol's followers would feel honoured, and agree: then the Incas had not only pleased a subject group, they also possessed that group's chief object of worship as a hostage.

One of their techniques for defusing the rebelliousness of conquered chiefs operated on the same principle. They would invite a chief to send his son to Cuzco to receive a royal education. Flattered by the honour, the chief would accept; and then his heir was safely in Inca hands as a hostage. But also as one who would grow up as an Inca, so that his loyalty could be relied on when he succeeded his father.

So although sun-worship was the state religion, it was far from the only one: it was rather the central religion, concentrated at the Navel.

Since its conquest in the sixteenth century, the Inca Empire has been seen as more or less despotic, but always as a hierarchy of great administrative sophistication and power. But now scholars are revealing a new picture: it was a heterogeneous society, not a uniform one. There wasn't one great pyramidal hierarchy in which all had their place. Rather, there was a wide spread of different peoples and tribes held together not so much by strict government as by their reciprocal exchange with the centre of the Empire. Villagers would give the Inca their time and labour by working certain days in his fields; in return he would give them food when they had none, and clothing and fiestas. So all the diverse subjects were in constant exchange with the imperial administration, the governors from Cuzco. This is why the meaning of Cuzco is so important: the forming principle of the Inca Empire was not fantastically different from that of earlier Andean kingdoms. It was built on the model of the Aymara Empire centered at Tiahuanaco, Stone in the Middle: the world had a centre, a navel, and the world was divided into four quarters which met at this navel. All the dispersed tribes could be united in one empire, because it had a centre. Take away the Navel, as the Spaniards did, and the Empire disintegrates.

With Cuzco, the Incas were able to raise vast labour forces for their great public works. The bridges, roads, forts, terraces and temples they built required huge teams, who trusted that what they did for the people of the Navel would be repaid. The fortress of Sacsayhuaman, for example, where Inti Raymi was held: each of its three walls is ten feet high and built of huge blocks of stone, some of them weighing over a hundred tons. Yet these great grey stones have been cut so accurately that you can't slip a knife between any of them. It must have taken millions of man-hours to build. Nor did it seem to the builders that they were constructing an instrument of their own domination: rather of their protection.

But now the fortress was swarming with people who had been sitting up on the walls to watch Inti Raymi. The display was over, and the crowd had spilled into the square to be close to the stage, where dances were being performed like the dances at Raqchi. There were plenty of vendors among the crowd: young boys with trays of cigarettes and sweets, Chola women with baskets and bowls of pastries which they covered with white tea-towels. The hills all about were dappled with the shadows of blustery clouds and the crowds were merry: the atmosphere had been released from the rhythmic oppressiveness of Inti Raymi. But I left it anyway: I had seen enough dancing.

I was walking down from the hill on which Sacsayhuaman is built, along a wide-worn path through a copse of eucalyptus, when suddenly a woman shrieked in English: 'There he is!'

Many other people were also descending into the city by this path, both Indians and gringos. The cry had come from above. I looked up. Just then a large American, in a puffed down jacket, came charging down the hill pushing people out of his way by their shoulders.

The same woman screamed: 'The one in purple!' And the man, with thundering paces, made for one of a group of mestizo youths who had stopped just below us to see what the commotion was. They were smiling. One caught my eye. Then the American hurled himself on to the group, landing on one who was wearing purple trousers, sending him crashing to the ground with the momentum of the downhill charge. Then, straddling the mestizo, he started punching him in the head and chest, shouting, 'Bastard! Bastard!' The other mestizos had drawn back. The woman came running down. She pointed to the captive youth: 'That's him. I swear. That's the one.' Her American voice was wrung high with emotion. Then, aware of all the people watching, she said, 'Yeah, he stole my wallet,' by way of explanation.

Her man had stopped beating the skimpy thief, and had pulled him to his feet by the scruff of the neck. The youth was whimpering in terror.

'Take him to the police,' the woman said. 'Okay, let's go.'

At this the thief's mouth opened involuntarily and he began to sob in high-pitched coughs. The man shook him violently, and walked him off, shoving from behind.

The other mestizos, his friends, watched in silence.

By the time I reached the Plaza de Armas the Procession of Effigies was about to begin. It was late afternoon. The square was thick with people. Three brass bands were making discord over the noise of the crowd. Occasional peals of laughter and shrieks of joy would rise through the din. The drinkers of the morning now staggered over the flowerbeds in the centre of the square; the drunks of the morning were draped over the myrtle hedges, unconscious and unnoticed. Beneath the bells of one of the brass bands a circle of Quechuas were stomping round and round. Two of them were playing Pan pipes inaudibly. Yet all the men, in flopping ponchos, trooped round energetically, taking the rhythm from the sight of the man ahead.

The Procession emerged from the Cathedral, four figures, three saints and the Virgin, held above the heads of the crowd. Two bishops in full regalia walked side by side in front of the Virgin. It took them over an hour to make their 300-yard circuit of the plaza. And though this procession was the climax of the Fiesta of Corpus Christi, it seemed incidental to the celebrations: nobody even got out of the way of the bishops. They had to force their way through. At times they made no headway at all.

I left the Plaza de Armas. Finally I had had my fill of fiestas. In a small plaza a hundred yards away there was a bar with tables on the pavement outside, in a colonnade. I ordered a beer, and sat watching the light fade. Opposite there was a building whose ground floor was built of Inca stones, as haphazard as crazy-paving in the shape of its blocks, but as tightly sealed as bricks and mortar in the joins between them. No earthquake has rocked an Inca wall, while all about the Spanish stones have tumbled.

I had the little plaza to myself. The din from the main square reached me as a low, continuous roar underlining the peace here.

I woke up to a grey dawn. A fine rain hung in the air. The streets were washed silver-grey. The Plaza de Armas, like a campfire in the morning, was ashes. The night's rain had put out the fire that blazed yesterday. The trestle tables stood sodden, decked with sodden chairs. One woman brushed pools of water from her table with a corner of her cardigan.

My car climbed out of Cuzco up the hills on its way to the Urubamba valley, the sacred valley of the Incas. Cuzco smouldered below. I was climbing up the eastern fence of the Altiplano. For once the sky was closed and white; I had a ceiling over my head: clouds blown up from the jungle in the east.

I stopped the driver when we reached the pass which would take us over the Cordillera. Behind, the hill rolled down into the Cuzco valley, and rose again beyond it soon to disappear in the mist. Turning my back on the Altiplano, the air of the jungle rose to my face, different from the high plain air even at this height. It was warm. It carried an exciting unfamiliar smell, of mud and river-weeds and fruit. I was close under the clouds here. Mists dangled beneath them. Below lay the Urubamba valley, a deep gulley chiselled into the Cordillera. At the bottom flowed the same river that passed Raqchi, the Vilcanota; but here it had come through its pass: there was no longer a barrier between it and the Amazon. The valley here is quite different from what it was upriver, in the highlands.

We wound back and forth, descending towards the little town of Pisac. Already the slopes were green with turf and boulders were covered with moss. Under the clouds, the valley might have been in Scotland. It was moorland. Ahead, on the far side, in a great half-bowl, were the terraces of Pisac, massive steps cut into the hill, each with a retaining wall of Inca masonry. And beneath them, amid a cluster of trees, was the town itself.

I didn't linger here. The 'traditional market' I had been told about consisted of several wealthy Chola women selling garishly dyed Andean clothes in small shops for the tourists.

Outside Pisac I sat on a wall to watch a long line of Quechua men and women work their way from end to end of a maize field, harvesting. Their huge field was held as a cooperative concern, so all had to do an equal share of the work. There must have been at least fifty of them plucking heads of corn among the plants. Andean maize grows to a height of four or five feet: only the harvesters' hats and shoulders were visible.

I took a bus further down the Urubamba valley, to Ollan-taytambo, a quiet village with Inca terraces and ruins above. Already the vegetation had changed: star-shaped rubbery plants with fat tendrils and shoots grasped on to cliff-faces; there were banana trees among the adobe houses, and avo-cado and orange trees. And here the clouds that came rolling up the valley hadn't yet massed against the Cordillera: they were loose fleeces scattered in the sky. Only occasionally did one stray across the sun. So the air here was quite different, thick and yellow with sunlight, warm, as if preparing to be very hot; and all around the dark green foliage glistened. Meanwhile, as we continued, the valley narrowed to a can-yon. What had been a dull river became a fast ruffled stream frequently breaking open over the rocks. Cliffs rose up on either side; somehow, on ledges, from cracks, tropical plants sprouted from the rockfaces. For the moist, sunny air was a powerful catalyst to fertility. It was as if here Pacha Mama could not be contained; or as if this were her very womb, bursting with plant life.

Is this why the Incas held the Urubamba valley sacred? Because they saw in it a wild fecundity unknown in the high-lands? Was it from this blazing display of nature, the air al-most visible, every plant glinting, that they derived their pageantry, their gold ornaments and richly coloured robes? For here the trinity that one scholar argues the Incas believed in—Inti the sun, Inti Illapata, fire, and Pacha Mama, the earth—are in harmony. Inti does not dry up Pacha Mama. He encourages her; together they make a blaze of dense colour, a flame of life, Inti Illapata. Was it this flaming, fertile air that the Incas held as sacred? *Quién sabe?* But one thing is known: the Incas fled to this valley when the Spaniards arrived in the highlands. Here they sought refuge.

Until the last decade Machu Picchu was believed to be the lost Inca city, Vilcabamba, where the Incas hid until they died out. Because archaeologists found many more female skeletons than male in Machu Picchu, they conjectured that the Sacred Virgins must have been brought here from Cuzco when the Spaniards were approaching. But now Machu Picchu has been shown almost undoubtedly not to have been the lost Vilcabamba: it was further down the valley, embedded in the jungle. Yet the ruins retain an air of peaceful seclusion.

Machu Picchu rests on a ridge one thousand feet above the Vilcabamba. The river turns a hairpin bend, so does the canyon, and on top of the arm of land about which they turn is the city, a sheer drop either side of it. It is a compact city, ingeniously built around various rocks protruding from the ground, with its own temple, plaza, sundial and terraces. It is a perfect, isolated, self-contained retreat for a small population. But its setting is the feature that has made it world-famous. It alone has probably done more for the Peruvian tourist industry than anything else. Behind it looms a huge peak draped in moss and foliage, like a person with a sheet over his head pretending to be a ghost. This is Huayna Picchu rising eerily over the masonry of the city.

Looking away, down the valley, over the steep mountains blanketed with tropical verdure, I was glad that the last Incas lived in the jungle. It had always fascinated them, for they were highland people unaccustomed to the ease of tropical life, to warm nights, plentiful shade, a bounty of fruits, deep rivers, None of the last three Inca emperors stayed to see the destruction of the way of life their fathers had built up in the Andes. Native civilization in the New World died out as it had grown up, isolated from the rest of the world.

But I only had half an hour in Machu Picchu before the first Americans of the day came puffing into the ruins, weighed down by cameras and videos and lenses and portable batteries.